Published by Mohit Pandey, 2015
Copyright© Mohit Pandey, 2015

Mohit Pandey has asserted his right under the Indian Copyrights Act 1957 to be identified as the author of this work.
This book is sold to the condition that it shall not, by way of trade or otherwise, be lent, resold, hired out, or otherwise circulated without the publisher's prior consent in any form of binding or cover other than that in which it is published and without a similar condition, including this condition, being imposed on the subsequent purchaser.

Vipreet Rajyoga – The Luck Unleashed
(Amazing Astrology)

By

Mohit Pandey

About the Author- A Professional Overview

Corporate Training Head India's Profile

Mr.Mohit Pandey is a young and talented professional after completing his Graduation with major specialization in Electronic-Commerce he had decided to switch over towards one of the most strange and prolific coupling of professions **Finance & Information Technology** by successfully attaining his Post Graduate qualification in **Business Finance** being an educational perfectionist with well-to-do academic records right through-out his career, from his alma martyr to his higher education where he cleared every academic session with reserved space in **merit list** ultimately routs towards the final destination for any financial sector aspirant and accomplish his Charter in finance **(Chartered Financial Analyst)** through the way of pursuing his **Doctorate** in **Finance** and perverted into Research And Development Department and associated with global brand name like **NIIT,G-Telsoft** and others.

His efforts and research work is crowned with the reorganization from an International Academic Promotion Company-**MMCS (Multiple Management Consultancy Services)** while he was working as **Business Research Analyst** for them, they have an agreement to run his training program & certifications in various wings of Finance which is consolidating totally into a new concept developed by Mr.Mohit Pandey termed as **Practical Finance.**

The finest feather in his cap has been added recently, When he worked as the **Central Government**

Representative in the State of Haryana at the Designation of **Financial Consultant**.

The Premium Educational The fine Institutes from developed countries like **UK, USA, GERMANY, IERLAND** and **many others** annexed with MMCS ltd. has bestowed the premium appreciation to his efforts.

Training camp along with the certification with maximum individual attention by experts is the cardinal base of **Fantastic Finance** rather than mere theory education which leaves the practical world at bay. To provide industry with ready professionals' proper practical training is indispensible.

In India his research work is approved by **INFOMAX** a **Non-Government-Organization** working with a bird's eye view on creating and providing superlative educational awareness and services at affordable price in each corner of the country and to every student of the country and had acquired his professional services while appointing him as **Financial Research Analyst** with an Italian job to design the training cum certification academic modules to groom-up India with the high profile educational professionals. As per Mr.Mohits views : All the financial charters ,courses ,degrees and other cling academic qualifications running has got no role to play in country's financial bill then even the lion's share of the most premium and high package career opportunities available is held by the financial sector only to become a financial analyst, investment banker or to held any-other specialization in this arena the life line requirement is knowledge and application as finance sector is ever-diversified and continuously changing the knowledge of process holds more practical significance than content.

Initially he was thinking of writing a book on Financial Analysis but somehow he induced to write a practical book on supernatural phenomenon. As he was equally inclined towards the science and the unknown and by profession an analyst he uses all his experience to build up a common platform in between the paranormal entities and logical explanations about them.

It is me or Is it me?

Astrology huh a useless topic isn't it? Who believes in such stupidities man? How stars or planets can so far away decides the destiny of an individual?

Many such questions you can often hear and you will have no explanation but this is true that successful individuals have separate breeds as every hardworking person doesn't taste success.

As far as my interest in Astrology is considered it has a very strange tale to narrate. I was a firm non believer in this wing of Vedas, predicting future but astrology has proven to be a tool for me to understand myself. Having diversified qualities in academics, sports, love life and other arenas of life I was still not happy and without knowing the exact reason.

Hunting for my unknown fears I had started digging into the Vedas, puranas and other related books and came to know that I am a Capricorn ascendant and these guys are past life sinners and no matter how much high they climb in life they can never be happy or satisfied. This was just a beginning, with the passage of time I had started researching on astrology since my schooldays and today I have got a different tune to play. The less or I should say the least known entity of Vedic Astrology the Vipreet RajYogas. It defines the breed of the winners, champions are born, born to be rich, to be successful and rise to sky from dust. Vipreet Rajyoga is not just mere Hrsha, Sarla and Vimla yogas , this concept can be elaborated far beyond this. Amazing Astrology is a series of book which will give you deep dip into the real and practical sense of astrology. Ask me why writing on astrology when you fiction books are doing well (I am a fiction writer also and written few horror books also mainly Beyond Lights The Darkness Knocks, Beyond Lights Shadows Of The Darkness, A Tale Of Ten Candles and Dark Tales are main among them), my answer is simple I have written this book for myself not for others and for those who consider astrology as their passion. We only do in this world for what God has made us and he gives us ways, resources and ability to achieve the heights pre decided for us irrespective of our present conditions. So enjoy the secret behind the unleashed luck and if you wish you can follow my links below –

Amazing Astrology

It is said the somewhere far away in the space when planets, nakshatras and other heavenly bodies change their movements the lives of the mortals on earth also change. All through my little life till now I always use to wonder about the superiority among the two words -Chance and Choice or in other words you can say Bhagya or Destiny and Karma or Action.

Is really our actions decides our destiny or our destiny decides our actions? Perhaps the answer to this question will never be found. But with the observations and little experience I have in my life I came to the conclusion that life is a cocktail of both luck and labor.

There is one very interesting story which I want to share with you and which will make my concept of combination very clear.

In a jungle there were three lions, one is lucky but lazy other is hard working but unlucky and the third has a little bit of both.

The first one is sleeping inside his cave and even after hearing the sounds of animals to hunt he is not getting up to grab what luck is serving to him so he is hungry.

The second lion is very hard working, he is hunting for food in mountains ,woods and everywhere but to his bad luck he is not getting any prey so he is also hungry.

The third lion has seen a deer at a bit more than normal distance from him but he had a long chase and finally his hard work was rewarded by the lady luck and he captured the deer and had his food.

So, what I want to say that the involvement of hard work and luck both is require to complete the picture and more the lucky you will be less the hard work will require to achieve your aims.

Luck provides you chance and hard work develops the capability to cash that chance for instance there are two farmers one is very hard working and other is lazy. The hard working one plough the land, put seeds into the ground and did all sorts of hard work which he could and now it depends upon weather to let him reap the benefits of his efforts if there will be good rain he will get good crops in case of adverse climatic changes he will suffer but the other lazy one did nothing so whether there will be rain or no rain he will get nothing because he didn't made any efforts to cash the possible chances.

But there are some extreme cases in which luck alone has the power to give heights of success to an individual and that too all of a sudden and in this book I am going to discuss about those most important but least discussed Yogas in Vedic Astrology.

As an astrologer a person can only assigned probabilities of predictions and until and unless more than 108 astrology considerations analyzed one can never be sure about an outcome of his prediction but yes this is also true that astrology is a science as old as the creation of universe and it also follows certain thumb rules.

This book is first in the series of my book series – Amazing Astrology in which I will try to expose the practical and logical face of Vedic Astrology as well as highlight certain veiled topics or less discussed themes in astrology.

From an individual's Kundali (Birth Chart) it is possible to tell that when, how and how much he will gain or lose in life and yes there are remedies effective enough to amplify the gains and minimize loss.

One thing I want to make you crystal clear that no remedy can change your luck completely, they had their limitations, no matter whichever gemstone you wear or whichever ritual you do the limit of luck alteration is 25%-30% which means that if you will have to loose 100 rupee you will lose 75 and if you will have to gain 100 rupee you will gain 125. If an astrologer could have changed the destiny of any individual than the first person would be he himself and every astrologer would have been millionaire whatever is in your fate you will get that only and if anything can change your fate then that is your own Karmmas(hard work).

When we analyze the auspicious Yogas (Conjunctions, aspects and nakshatras in particular position) the first name comes to everyone's mind is Raj Yoga, Raj Yoga which led the person to live successful life with affluent resources at his disposal but when we go deeper into the Astrology secrets, men who merges his actions into the sea of fate and came out with unique pearls are very few. For example-Lord Buddha, Napoleon, Alexander the great, Mahatma Gandhi, Mark Zuckberg ,Sachin Tendulkar and many more who just turned their fate around and reached hundreds and thousands times over and above their previous level are very few where as Raj Yogas you can found in the Kundalis of Lakhs and Lakhs of people.

So, where lays the difference?

It indicates that there are certain Yogas in Vedic Astrology which are not only beyond Raj Yogas but also far more powerful and highly active than them, they have ability to take a normal human to outstanding level and a good for nothing individual to best for everything stage and major of such yogas are-

First - Neech Bhanga Raj Yoga (Cancellation Of Weakness)

Second – Vipreet Raj Yoga (Turn Of Fates or Reversal of fortune)

It was both a bit shocking and surprising for me that on internet there are countless articles available which explains Neech Bhanga Rajyoga and its attributes and effects but almost everywhere Vipreet Rajyoga has been considered as a mere stroke of luck and some half logics like Vipreet Rajyoga needs to have supporting Rajyogas to sustain the success and blah blah blah whereas the reality is this that Vipreet Rajyoga has all the qualities of Neech Bhanga Rajyoga with couple of additional advantages over it- It brings great success without much efforts or no efforts at all and it brings success timely unlike in Neech Bhanga Rajyoga where the person although gets great success but after a long and hard struggle.

This book contains the in depth analysis of Vipreet Rajyoga concept with its applications in different lagnas(ascendants) and with example of analyzed kundalis of great persons having this unique Yoga in their Kundalis.

Basics of Astrology-

Before we start our extended stroll towards the practical astrology and the deep analysis of the offbeat yoga which are at the superlative stage as compare to Raj Yogas we must discuss some of the basics of Astrology.

For any predictions to be accurate the accuracy of the followings are required-

1. Birth Chart should be correct.

2. The accurate analysis of the twelve houses of birth chart

3. The zodiac signs in the twelve houses and positions of their depositors.

4. Aspects and conjunctions of different planets.

5. Yogas or combinations or connections of planets into the Birth Chart

It is a scientific assumption that almost all the heavenly bodies in universe are round like planets and stars. If we take Sun as the center point and our solar system as a whole universe then it will also form a very large circle.

And as per the attributes of circle the full circle always denotes 360 degrees and now we divide those 360 degrees among the twelve zodiac signs and it will come as 360/12= 30, so the optimum level of any planet is from 0 to 30 degrees*.

Note-We will discuss the scenario of degrees in the upcoming chapters.

Sun although is a stable planet but it has the most vital effect on the birth chart.

As per the attributes of our earth and the position of Sun the every living and non-living object on planet earth are mostly effected by the zodiac sign which is rising on the eastern horizon which is called the *Udya Rashi* or the rising sign of zodiac or ascendant in your birth chart.

In other language that Zodiac Sign is your Lagna or Ascendant which is the base of your birth chart and the most important sign in your birth horoscope the strong Ascendant Lord can quote any miracle on planet earth for an individual no matter if other planets are weak.

The Lagna is the first house of your birth chart and the other zodiac sign follows it.

For example if you are Capricorn Lagna born then the number in the first house of your Kundali (Birth Chart) will be 10 and in the second house it will be 11 and so on.

As an astrologer whatever the little knowledge I have gained the core outcome of it is this, that as an astrologer one can assign the probabilities of events by looking at the birth chart but accurate predictions can only be made after reading out the divisional charts only in which I give the highest weightage to Navmansha Chart or the D-9 chart.

As I have already told you that Birth chart is the map of our solar system at the time of the birth of an individual and Kundali is universe's way to communicate our purpose of life on earth.

The earth is a spinning sphere and within 24 hours it crosses all the twelve zodiac signs and an individual if goes through his *Purna Aayu* or complete life it goes through the *Mahadashas* (Major Time Periods), *Anter Dashas* (Sub time periods), *Pratyanterdashas* (Minor time periods) and *the Sukshma Dasha* or little time periods occurred in a day which effects the outcome of *Karmas* or actions of an individual in positive or negative way.

Karma is the first priority as only 0.002% of individuals have such a strong horoscope to get everything they desired through sheer luck but still if we analyze their birth charts then the *Purva Punya Sthans* or Past life good deeds houses (1 st, 5th and Navmansha Chart) turns out to be strong so whatever they are getting is still the outcome of their own actions but in past life and *Veepreet Rajyoga* is the best example of such yogas which give success in a jiffy to a person but yes at the cost of the loss of other individual or individuals like if anyone invent an outstanding model of automatic washing machine and grab the full share of this market then the other sellers will be at loss, if a person wins a big lottery then others who had purchased the lottery will be at loss and many more such examples but Vipreet Rajyoga doesn't finishes here it has a prolonged way to go depending on the following situations-

- The mode of its creation

- The house of creation

- Exchange Analysis

- Coupled with Neech Bhanga Rajyoga or not.

Sub Division of Kundali or Birth Chart-

As it is already mentioned that First House or the lagna or Ascendant is the most important house in your horoscope now we move towards the other important houses in an individual's birth chart.

- Kendra or Quadrant houses-

1st,4th,7th and 10th house are called Kendras. They basically denotes the four directions of our universe and said to be the common Place of Supreme Lord Shree Mahavishnu (One of the deity of Hindu trilogy). They said to be the benefic houses and specifically the houses of satisfaction.

Whether a person will be satisfied with the commodities and relations related to these houses in his life it can be predicted by analyzing these houses.

- Trikonas or Tri houses –

1st,5th and 9th house are called the Tri houses or the houses forms the triangle to connect all the twelve houses in Kundali or birth chart.

Note-First house or lagna is counted as both Kendra and Trikona and that is why it is the most important house in your kundali or birth chart.

These houses are 5th from each other so forms the most strong flow of energy and are the most benefic houses in your horoscope as they indicates success and said to be the common place for Shree Maha Laxmi Maa (Mother of wealth and prosperity and wife of Shree Maha Vishnu in Hindu Mythology)

Tri houses indicate changes and construction in an individual's life how much their life can change either positive or negative can be predicted by analyzing these houses.

Kendra Vs Trikona-

A conjunction of Kenra and Trikona Lords always bring success with satisfaction or if only Kendra lord is strong the person will be satisfied with whatever he has and if only tri lord is strong then the person will never be satisfied no matter whatever he will gain in life.

Evil Houses- 6th, 8th and 12th are said to be the most evil houses or DustAsthanas in Kundali.

They indicate the enemies,diseases,death and sufferings in the old age all in all only bad things about and individual and the lord of these houses when they goes into other houses they always destroy the results of that particular house for example if lord of the 6th house which indicates diseases,debt etc. goes into the 9th house the most benefic house in kundali it will make the person miss the strokes of good luck like good opportunities of education,profession etc. by putting the hurdles like sudden disease, loans etc. and subsided the good outcome of 9th house.

Zodiac Signs in the houses-

As it has been already told one zodiac sign holds 0-30 degrees and 12 zodiacs completes 12*30=360 degrees so in a particular house which Zodiac will fall with what the degree wise strength it effects the outcome of that particular house.

The nature of the planet sitting in lagna will dominate the person's inherent nature for his whole life time like if lagna or first house contains male planet then the person will be dominating, if it contains fire sign he will be aggressive by nature, if water sign then very calculative and sharp minded and so on so now we first get familiar with the houses of kundali.

The First House-

The First House or Lagna is usually mentioned to be the House of Self. The cusp of the First House is the home of the Ascendant, the sign that was rising on the eastern horizon at the precise moment of one's birth. The rational outcome of this in terms of sunrise denotes the new beginning and new beginnings; one begins of a new life on planet earth to hold the notions of the First House.

The new beginnings here are pinpointed to you: the self and the associated journey of discovery that define a person. Who are you? What will you become? How you will look like? What your general health will be? How do you realize your best self? The First House speaks to the understanding of one's ultimate latent. This procedure of flattering a sole individual is one of the greatest gifts we make to the world in which we are living today.

The distinct qualities that we possess are often referred to as 'personality'. The First House addresses the individual and their comportment and approach to life. In other words, the sum total of one's being. This is the package we give to the world. The packaging itself, or our outer being, is also governed by the First House -- the physical body and the way in which we present ourselves and, in particular, the head and face.

The Lagna also rules early babyhood. Everything from our first few steps to our view of the emerging world is measured here. How will we develop? What is our view on life? It all begins at the beginning (the First House) and serves to shape us for all time. If you have Lagna lord or any of his friendly planets or exalted planet sitting in your lagna then no matter how bad your kundali will be somehow you will see through all the hurdles but for this degree wise strength of the planet is mandatory.

All in all the first house is you yourself and a strong lagna is the most important fact in Vedic Astrology
The First House is ruled by Aries and the planet Mars which is the owner and Sun is the natural Karka (Most active planet) of first house.

Some default placements for First house are as follows-

- If the zodiac falls in the first house is Gemini, Virgo, Libra or Aquarius then it is considered to be strong.

- If you have Lagna lord or any of his friendly planets or exalted planet sitting in your lagna then no matter how bad your kundali will be somehow you will see through all the hurdles but for this degree wise strength of the planet is mandatory

- If there are two or more than two planets in the first house they will be termed as female planets as both the owner and the karaka of first house are Sun and Mars which are male planets.

- It is a natural most benefic house in Kundali.

- It is counted among both Kendra (quadrant) and Trikona (trine).

- The natural owner Mars and Karka or most active planet Sun are best friends of each other.

Second House-

It is also termed as the house of Wealth, possession and money. It also denotes our family.

Precise belongings covered by the Second House comprise earned income and our ability to affect it, investments and portable property (cars, clothing, jewelry and other likewise things). Debt is also part of the calculation here, since we own the responsibility to pay our bills. How we view money, the acquisition of wealth (and debt), financial reversals, savings, budgeting and financial status are all ruled by the Second House.

If it is positive you will be capable of paying off your debts if negative you will earn the money but will hardly save anything or utilize that money for yourself that is why second house needs the support of eleventh house as it is fourth from eleventh house or a Kendra or quadrant from eleventh house which led to money which brings satisfaction..

It defines your vocal skills,good looks,eye,nose,ear,singing ability.

It is the own house of Jupiter or Jupiter is its Karaka and it belongs to Taurus the self-sign of Venus the natural owner of second house so the two most beneficial planets-Jupiter and Venus gets co active in second house if your second house is strong you will be able to pay of your family debt by fulfilling your responsibilities and earn lots of moveable wealth in your life.

- Second house is said to be a neutral house which means if it will have friendly planets it will give great results and if it will have enemy planets it will give bad results as the Natura owner Venus and Natural Karka Jupiter despite of being the most beneficial planets are the arch enemies of each other that is why the lord of the second house is also known as the Pratham Markesh (First cause of death) and thus in considering Vipreet Rajyoga under specific circumstances the second house also has its role.

Third House-

Third house is the house of communication, action, bravery, patience, vulvar, servants, Yoga, cough and breathing problems. The zodiac is Gemini and it is ruled by Mercury and its natural Karka is Mars.As mercury is a neutral planet and Mars is a male and fiery planet so Mercury is unable to give much results in this house, so it is dominated by Mars.

Majority of the communication is going on amongst the individual and those he or she holds close ties with like brothers and sisters, as well as neighbors, servants, friends etc.. Although communication here can be both written and verbal, it also has a aware class to it so third house is also the house of intelligence.

Early schooling, efficiently teaching us how to think and interconnect, is also covered by the Third House, as are short trips. Again, the adjacent nature of travel speaks to the near nature of the Third House: those we know well, in our atmosphere, keeping that environment constricted.

Note- Third house is somewhat a bad house as it also signifies ups and downs in an individual's life although being sixth house from the eighth it also destroys the bad effects of the eighth house and if Saturn or mars is placed in this house they save the person from sudden dangers only as the natural owner of this house Mercury has a little say in his own house and as it is dominated by a natural cruel planet the good outcomes of the third house is always under hurdle so it also comes into the play of partial Vipreet Rajyoga under specific situations.

Fourth House-

The first sole Kendra or quadrant house as Lagna or first is counted in both trine and Kendra houses.

It denotes to the Sukh Bhava or the house of Satisfaction.It signifies happiness, parental happiness,mother,house,immovable goods,gardnes,cattle,mercy,donations and stomach of an individual.

It is ruled by Moon and it is a natural benefic house.

Fifth House-

Fifth House is said to be the house of happiness and pleasure, it also signifies creative intelligence, education (specifically graduation), guidelines in life, devotion to god, children, management abilities, Maternal uncle, regular earnings, sudden earnings, job, fame, gall bladder, earnings of children, services and care by children.

Frequently pleasure is the result of a creative performance. The modest act of creating is, essentially, giving of oneself and making something -- making additional. Fifth House though speak to breeding and children, but it also addresses the creation of art and culture and new life on earth. The artistic life is one from which we can originate much personal desire and complacency.

Romance and romantic affairs, both are the forms of expressive pleasures, are within the kingdom of the Fifth House. Expressive gratification can be enlarged in many ways, and yet another way addressed by this House is gambling. Though this implies a financial risk, it can also be viewed as the willingness to take a risk as well as gaining sudden wealth -- on love, with money or in life. A calculated risk in the expectations of a enjoyable outcome is how the Fifth House gets it.

The Zodiac or this house is Leo and the Natural Ruler is Sun and the most active planet of the natural karka of fifth house is the best friend of Sun is Jupiter.

It is also a complete benefic house.

Sixth House-

It is the first sole evil house not bad but evil or the house which can only give bad results under the normal circumstances.

The sixth house is termed as the house of health, adversity, enemies, doubts, worries ,property, Maternal Uncle's health, hips. As mortal beings, we obviously have inadequacies to have no control over the natural or sudden difficulties. What will we do with them? How will we react in the face of a individual crisis? Crises, illnesses and reversals of fortune are all part of our mortal life.

It is also the house of fear- The fear of losing job, the fear of diseases and enemies but once an individual crosses this barrier of fear after fear there will be a fantastic life for him.

It is ruled by Virgo owned by Mercury and the most active planet or natural karka is Ketu (Tail of serpent),Mercury is a natural neutral planet and Ketu is a shadow planet a headless but immense energy and both of these planets depends upon other planets for results as they both are identityless so if the sixth lord creates Vipreet Rajyoga it give tremendous benefits specially in business which involves communication(mercury) and energy (ketu).Ketu and mercury both also indicate decision making power if supported by the well placed sixth lord of the particular ascendant or lagna they can make a person billionaire in a jiffy very beneficial placement.

It is a natural Evil House.

Seventh House-

It is the house of Marriage, Sexual desires, sex relations, partnerships, quarrels and gain through partners (both marriage partner and business partners).

The owner of this house is Venus and the natural karka are both Venus and Mercury as it has two karkas it creates confusion and unnecessary fears and failures sometimes in personal relations and professional life but all in all a benefic house as Mercury is a good adapter of the owner of this house Venus.

It also indicates the loyalty and character of your life partner.

It has some evil attributes also that is why despite of being Kendra it is also the first house of life threat and house of Dritiya Markesh (Second cause of death) and under some very rare conditions it also contributes to Vipreet Rajyogas.

Eighth House-

As Ninth house is considered to be the most benefic among trines and a table turner for an individual as it is the house of luck and Mool Trikona(self Centre point) of an individual's birth chart or kundali the eighth house is considered to be the most evil and worst house and the center point of the Dusthasthanas or the Evil houses in kundali.

It indicates an individual's life,personal secrets,lies,sudden events,death and its causes,mental disorders,hidden wealth,hidden talent,past life out comes,rebirth,occult,magic,secret sex relations,overseas travels,private body parts and materialistic benefits from in-laws.

It is owned By Mars and natural Karkas or most active planets are both Mars and Saturn, the two completely opposite forces and arch enemies of each other that is why it is also called the Randra Bhava, being the worst house of kundali in case of Vipreet Rajyoga it gives most unexpected and grand results specially in terms of combination of wealth and fame,a fame which becomes immortal even after this mortal life as the lord of the eighth house is the planet which effects the Arudha Lagna of an individual to great extent so you may be something else but your public image will be completely different and your secrets are well served.

Inveterate to this House's importance on sex, it's significant to memo that the French refer to an orgasm as 'le petit mort' or 'the little death.' When we grasp that high state of intimacy, we leave a little of ourselves behind -- die a small death. One can also have a contradicting mode to view this as a new beginning, the rebirth of the soul or a gain for the partnership. The Eighth House is an equal-opportunity house, placing sex, death and rebirth on the same level playing field and recognizing the feasibility and importance of all three. We will all have involvement death and rebirth as part of our lives consciously or sub-consciously,failed relationships leading to new partners, end of old job let to hunt for better one, a new hairstyle. We are regenerated and reborn with each new phase and should welcome them.

Joint possessions also fall within the Eighth House like inheritance, alimony, taxes, insurance and support from another. Financial support, as well as spiritual, emotional and physical support, are spoken by this house.

It is basically the house of transformation from old to new.

It is the worst house of Kundali.

The Ninth House-

The strongest among all the trine houses and the Mool Trikona sign of the kundali the real table turner among the good houses and capability to rise the person from normal to extra normal level in a little span of time it is the house of father,luck,fortune,Dhrama (the right),philosophy, higher education, purposeful overseas travels, past life good deeds, worship, psychological advancement, white magic and real outcome of your marriage.

The Ninth House retells us that we are on a journey of detection. Along that road, we will come face-to-face with our ideals and further figure our integrities. Additional method to a richer understanding of life and more significantly, of the indefinite, is through spirituality. Understanding and accepting that which is superior to us, and our world, is key to the Ninth House.

The manner in which we enlarge our internal and external lives is also spoken by the Ninth House. Travel and communication with other peoples and philosophies ,different customs are a means to this end. Our dreams -- those that demonstrate our past as well as those that speak to future events -- also help to mildew our being and our associations.

A strong Ninth house can only be gained in three ways-

1. The good deeds in past life

2. Good deeds of your father

3. Divine blessings of your Kul Devata (Family God)

It is owned by Jupiter and the most active planet is also Jupiter so under the complete possession of the biggest planet in our solar system it can move freely and give results in optimum ways and level.

It is the most benefic house in kundali.

Tenth House-

This is the Kendra for an individual's legal rights,luxuries,fame,leadership,authority,status,government,high profile jobs, parental business all in all a house of social status. Bones diseases, cough, lungs are also considered by this house.

It is the strongest among the Kendra houses or quadrants as It is also both ruled and activated by Saturn which is the natural owner and Most active Planet of this house, the zodiac is Capricorn and the house is the house of highest activities and achievements.

Vocation is vital in the Tenth House. What role will we select and how will we best fill it? How much do we want to achieve? And how far you will be successful in it, Career, professional goals, ambition and motivation all encircled by the tenth house. In a more practical context, companies and their rules are enclosed here, as are any other administrations (specifically the government) that have the ability to rule over us. Along with our life's work comes the trial of ruling over others, although there will generally be someone who lords over us.

It is also a great signifier of Arudha Lagna or fame the person will achieve in life.

It is the benefic house among quadrants or kendras.

Eleventh House-

This house denotes assets (both fixed and liquid),luxuries, good deeds, veichles, gemstones, friends, society contribution, big brother, profits and over all desires.

It is owned by Saturn and the Zodiac sign is Aquarius and the most active planet or Natural Karka of the eleventh house is Jupiter and Saturn. Despite of all these good attributes it is also termed as a neutral house which depends upon the planet's placements to deliver its results because the owner and the karka if not enemies then even holds opposite attributes but similar guidelines.

Jupiter is the natural magnifier it expands whatever it touches the qualities, the outcomes etc. whereas Saturn signifies limitations and boundaries, Jupiter is the indicator of divine immortal light and Saturn denotes the limitless darkness but setting these differences asides these planets gives results to an individual as per their actions or deeds Jupiter delivers it quickly and Saturn with a delay so eleventh house is very important .

The Eleventh House is usually mentioned to as the House of Networks and groups also,Through our friends and social network, we find strength in numbers -- we see the power of the cooperative, the cluster. Groups spoke by this house include clubs, organizations, social groups, schmoozing organizations and professional associations. The emphasis here is on the actions we undertake within these groups, how we make a difference and as a result, how we grow and actualize our true selves. The popular leaders and famous personalities and businessmen also need to be a good manager of networks.

Our expectations and dreams, what we want and what we need to achieve. Our original vision is painted, the simple act of working toward our greatest selves. The power of shared creation, as well as the creative sparks caused by the group, are also important to this house. By banding together, we can create so much more.

The house signifies support from powerful individuals or from common mass.

Eleventh House also governs stepchildren, foster children and adopted children.

It also signifies Vipreet Raj Yoga under certain circumstances.

Twelfth House-

The final destination of life. It is the house of loss,expenditure,punishments,addiction,diseases,donations,external affairs, old age ,secrets (the secrets which has been kept from you),Unconsciousness and after life.

The unconscious state can aid in producing our successes, as well as contribute us in handling with our failures. Success vs. failure: do we deliberately challenge our lives or subconsciously sweep things under the familiar rug? This house might more aptly be called the House of Calculation, since it is in the Twelfth that we review what we have been (and done) and decide where we go from there. Along with these unconscious reflections, we also cautious on strengths and weaknesses that are hidden from public view.

Your coming rebirth can be predicted by this house.

It is the house which defines our final personality and ultimate achievements through subconscious development we will be able to defeat our enemies or overcome the challenges in life or not is decided by this house.

The Zodiac sign is Pieces and it is ruled by Jupiter while the natural Karka or the most active planet is an arch enemy of Jupiter Rahu.

Rahu the head of the serpent without stomach so it will eat but never satisfied and Jupiter which holds no attachment to materialistic success a cocktail if gets right can give you extra normal wealth but no satisfaction.

This is an evil house and contributes to Vipreet RajYoga to great extent in kundalis.

One thing must be coming into your minds as it had always stricken my mind whenever I use to read the articles on astrology by other authors but nobody has explained this,today I am taking the liberty to elaborate this one of the most important but never explained concept of Vedic Astrology which forms the key stone of the good, neutral and evil houses in kundali for you-

What is the difference between the owner of the house and Natural Karka or the most activated planet?

Owner of the house – Owner of the house is the planet which has utmost control over any house, it is all in all the core ruler of that house and he can do good or bad simply anything depends on his own wish, just like if you are an owner of a big bungalow and you have a big drawing room but you want to keep your bed their. It is practically wrong but as the house belongs to you so you can do anything.

For example in Indian cricket team caption Dhoni can make a lower order batsman to open whether other team members are pleased with it or not, so what I want to make you understand is that the owner of the house or sign can run that particular house at his free will that is the solo reason why the position of the lord of the house in the Kundali or birthchart is so very important.

Say it is my house and I want to sleep in the bathroom, I know it is wrong but my wish is foremost whatever I do is right in my house.

Karaka or Best Planet in the house – It is the least explained but most important topic of Vedic astrology. What will happen if you are a civilian and you will became an owner of a jungle?, Another example is what if you are a habitant of a rural area and you became an owner of most modernize building with lifts, automatic systems complex to operate ?

What I meant to say is being owner alone doesn't make you strong or comfortable; you must possess the right thing. A hockey stick is as useless for Sachin Tendulkar as a cricket bat to Maradona.

Sachin is best with cricket bat, Maradona with football, A software engineer with laptop and a farmer with farming tools.

This is what the Natural Karka or the best planet in the house mean, the planet which can utilize the best qualities of a particular house to the utmost, a planet which exhales its energy most positively in particular house, the champion of that arena, the well known to that house, just like you purchase a big mansion and become the owner but an old servant who has been living in that mansion from past 25 years, he knows better than you about that house.

To make myself clearer I am quoting another example – The caption of Indian cricket team is M.S.Dhoni but the best player is Virat kohli

Ultimate outcome – When team can do well?, it's caption is strong or It's best player is strong or both?

Take another example from cricket only as in India it is the most popular game so it will be easy for everyone to know my view. Say M.S.Dhoni the caption don't like Virat Kohli so he makes him bat low down the order when Virat has very little chances to perform or in another example Virat Kohli secretly hates M.S.Dhoni so regardless of of the fact that Dhoni makes Virat open the batting to provide him maximum chance to perform, Virat willfully downgrades his game and play a wet blanket rather than a match winner, so the net result will be a failure.

You have given some other work to your servant who knows your newly owned mansion very well so he will not be able to perform the task given by you or he secretly don't like you so willingly serves you bad.

This is what which is the exact cause behind the good bad and neutral houses.

Now say M.S.Dhoni and Virat Kohli are very good friends and they complement each other very well so what will happen?, M.S.Dhoni will give best opportunities to Virat to perform and Virat will give his best performance to M.S.Dhoni and ultimately the performance of the team will enhance.

Now let us see the houses, their owners, and their natural karkas, the relationship in between the owner and the Karka and the result of the house in kundali or Natal charts.

House	Owner	Natural Karka or Best Planet	Relationship	Nature of House
First House	Mars	Sun	Best Friends	Most important house
Second House	Venus	Jupiter	Competitive Rivals and most benefic planets	Neutral house as ruled by most benefic but rival planets so termed as first Markesh also.
Third House	Mercury	Mars	Mercury kept secret friendship with Saturn the arch enemy of Mars.	Neutral house but sometimes evil planets perform well.
Fourth House	Moon	Moon	Solo owner	One of the best houses
Fifth House	Sun	Jupiter	Close friends	Benefic house a trine house
Sixth House	Mercury	Ketu (Tail of serpent)	Mercury a neutral planet and Ketu a shadow planet so indicates	Evil house

			sudden diseases ,enemies etc.	
Seventh House	Venus	Venus and Mercury	Having two Karkas but having more under the effect of Venus it is a good house but as Mercury is a neutral planet and will get effected by the positions of other planets in Kundali or birth chart so it is also the house of second Markesh	Good house but yet can give bad results under specific circumstances and hence can also give Vipreet Rajyogas under specific positions.
Eighth House	Mars	Mars and Saturn	Worst house as the owner and Natural Karka are core enemies and planets of exactly opposite	Worst House

			qualities.	
Ninth House	Jupiter	Jupiter	Solo ownership of Jupiter	Best House, the strongest trine
Tenth House	Saturn	Saturn	Solo Ownership of Saturn	Strongest Quadrant or Kendra, very benefic house.
Eleventh House	Saturn	Saturn & Jupiter	Good house but sometimes bad as Saturn and Jupiter holds natural ties but not friends exactly so position of other planets decides its outcome	Benefic house but can be evil also
Twelfth House	Jupiter	Rahu or head of serpent	Enemy owner and Natural Karka	Evil House

So things to observe in the above chart is all the strong and benefic houses has solo ownership of House owner and natural karka.

Fourth house has Moon it is the house of no enemies as it is also the house of mother and even the most evil person on earth will never get bad to his mother, Ninth house which is owned and controlled by Jupiter ,the biggest planet in our solar system, it is the owner and karka of ninth house and thus making it the house of luck or game changer and now tenth house which is owned by Saturn and Saturn is its natural Karka, it is strongest of the quadrant houses, the house of highest action level.

In Vedic astrology the ownership of the houses in Kundali or Natal chart changes with every lagna but the inherent qualities of the houses will remain the same, 25 percent of the house effect will always be there despite of the lagna or ascendant or zodiac quality.

Just consider that if soul of a dog incarnate a body of the human then what will happen?, Although taken birth as a human but that man's intrinsic quality will be of a dog only, therefore houses or bhavas are the soul of the depositor planets.

Planets- Planets are the celestial spheres moves freely in the space rotating around sun following their orbits caused by the unknown universal magnetic field and known magnetic power of Sun and in this book I will try to explain how, why and which planets can cause strong Vipreet Rajyogas.

Sun-

Sun is the center point and the guideline creator of our Solar System, if we consider our solar system as the whole universe then Sun is the eye of that Universe. Sun is a male planet and considered to be a cruel planet but not evil.

Note-A cruel planet and an Evil planet are not the same, an individual under the effect of cruel planets holds no mercy to sinners where as an individual under the effect of evil planets will be bad to good person also, deception, betrayals etc. will be his natural tendencies.

Sun owns the east direction and he is of fiery nature, The king of the planets and all other planets rotates around him.It is a male planet with warrior qualities and it denotes Aura, Soul,Respect,Government,Ruler,Bravery and Anger.

Moon, Jupiter and Mars are his best friends and Venus,Rahu (Head Of Serpent, Ketu (Tail of Serpent and Saturn are his arch enemies whereas Mercury is neutral.

Deity Of Sun-Supreme Lord Shree Maha Vishnu

When it forms the Vipreet Rajyoga it tends to give an individual a sense of bravery to challenge the difficult circumstances, established social customs and his own inherent nature to change his luck and life very rapidly, Sun when forms the Vipreet Rajyoga gets full support of all other planets as being their king after all.

But anyhow it is a Divine planet with harsh attributes so the Vipreet Rajyoga created through Sun brings more fame than wealth, a sudden

and immortal fame person gets to live beyond his life through his works.

Moon – Moon is the indicator of Mind, emotions, Mother, social relationships. It also governs water and tides and its biggest uniqueness is, it is the closest planet to earth so it has very quick effect on your birth chart or Kundali.

Silver, white cloths and others, the deity of moon is Lord Shree Mahadeva (One of the trinity of Hinduism).

Sun and Mercury are good friends and Rahu, and Ketu are enemies where as Saturn,Mars,Venus and Jupiter are neutral towards it. Being the fastest moving planet Moon holds much more importance and that is the reason why in Vedic Astrology Moon birth chart holds substantial water. If moon is waxed or benefic in your birth chart is will be a good planet and if malefic than evil planet.

Vipreet Rajyoga by Moon is balanced one great combination money and fame and usually through one of the better ways as compared to Vipreet Rajyogas from other planets.

If Moon creates Vipreet Rajyoga in a particular Birth Chart the effect will be exceptionally quick and smooth but it has the tendencies of subsiding down also quickly.

The fourth house is measured as the own house of Moon. It is exalted in the 1st, 2nd, 3rd, 4th, 5th, 7th and 9th houses and debilitated in the 6th, 8th, 10th, 11th and 12th houses.

Mars – Mars a warrior, a fighter, a merciless commander, the fearless, Is a natural cruel planets and sometimes evil to for some specific Lagnas but one good thing about Mars is ,it is an action hero and it has the tendencies to break the cardinal rules of traditional theories of Vipreet Rajyogas, as Vipreet Rajyogas are said to be governed by the adverse circumstances rather than personal efforts but a Vipreet Rajyoga created by Mars is inclined towards the personal aggression and not let go kind of attitude by an individual.

The 1st and 8th houses are the own houses of Mars and he gets exalted in the 10th house, and of his debilitation houses, Mars acts as a malefic in the 4th and 8th houses, but he is benefic if placed in the 1, 2, 3, 5, 6, 7, 9, 10, 11 and 12th houses.

Sun, Moon and Jupiter are its best friends and Venus and Saturn are worst enemies whereas Mercury, Rahu (head of the serpent) and Ketu (tail of the serpent) are neutral planets.

A Vipreet Rajyoga where the Mars came into play makes the most lazy and careless person the most active and attentive person at the most important moments. He just makes the hay while the sun shines leaving all, his adverse qualities and fears behind.

Vipreet Rajyoga follow numerous rules like no aspect of any good planet, no conjunction with any trine lord etc. to be fully fruitful but Vipreet Rajyogas created by Mars are only possibilities to make half chances full just like in a cricket match an outstanding catch can get you an impossible wicket, sometimes you go for such catches and other times those catches comes to you so all in all you cannot predict what Mars can do in its Vipreet Rajyogakaraka Dashas (Time of creation of Vipreet Rajyoga).

If someone remember the innings of M.S.Dhoni the Indian cricket team caption in world cup finals in which he played a match winning knock despite of being a flop player in the rest of the tournament.

It is somewhat like that doing your best at the most important moment to gain maximum gain from minimum effort of average efforts in the special situations in your life.

Mercury – The faceless planet, the prince, the communicator, the divine messenger, the forever child and many more qualities and attributes with which you can define Mercury.

Mercury has a very special and unique quality which no other planet holds in Vedic Astrology, Mercury is the only planet which has the capable of creating very strong Vipreet Rajyoga regardless of the dual ownership of signs.

For example if a planet holds the ownership of one dusthasthana or evil house (6th ,8th ,12th) and one trine (1st,5th or 9th house) at the same time then it cannot contribute to Vipreet Rajyoga as being the owner of one of the trines its evil qualities vanished and it will be considered as a Yogkaraka (good planet) rather than evil planet but Mercury can still create Vipreet Rajyoga if it sits with a naturally cruel or evil planet.

For example – For Capricorn Langna Mercury is the owner of 6th and 9th house, 6th an evil house and 9th the strongest trine then what will be the VipreetRajyoga conditions for Mercury in Capricorn Lagna?

If Mercury is in 6th house with Sun or Jupiter, in 8th house with Sun or Jupiter or in 12th house with Sun or Jupiter it will be a Vipreet Rajyoga regardless of the fact that Mercury is also a trine lord. Why?

Mercury is faceless, it has no identity it is a neutral planet but with a very special quality, it absorbs the qualities of the planets with which it sits and conjunction of Mercury with Sun or Jupiter which are the Lords of the 8th and 12th house respectively for Capricorn Lagna changes the qualities of Mercury from Yogkaraka (benefic planet) to Maraka (Evil planet).

Mercury is measured as auspicious in the 1, 2, 4, 5, 6 and the 7th houses and gives bad results when placed in the 3, 8, 9, 10, 11 and 12th. 7th house is the own house of Mercury. It stands exalted in the 6th house and gets debilitated in the 12th house

Note – Jupiter although the most beneficial planet in Vedic Astrology but only for Capricorn Lagna it is ati maraka (very malefic planet) as it owe two bad houses 3rd and 12th.

Vipreet Rajyogas created by Mercury usually comes from medical sources, communication technology, business and sometimes arts and one good thing about Mercury Vipreet Rajyoga is, it brings person joy and refreshments from their past troubles and it is the most satisfying of all the Vipreet Rajyogas created by other planets.

Jupiter – The teacher, The Philosopher, The Saint, The real Karka (cause) of luck. It is the biggest planet in our solar system and not only the biggest but the teacher of all the planets and yes the most important is it is the most benefic planet in Vedic Astrology.

Jupiter is considered more even more important than Sun the King as even the King also bow his head in front of his teacher. Being the most benefic planet the potential of Jupiter to provide very strong Vipreet Rajyoga subsided a little but at the same time the benefits derived from Vipreet Rajyoga created by Jupiter are everlasting and more important it gives spiritual satisfaction to an individual which is a consistently missing element in Vipreet Rajyoga.

The most vital element or quality of Jupiter is ,it is the magnifier or it multiplies or enhances the results of any particular yoga wither good or bad so if Jupiter sits with any evil or bad house lord in his debilitated sign or evil sign and the creates Vipreet Rajyoga which will be immense and beyond even the thinking of an individual.

Jupiter is exalted in the 4th house and the 10th house is the house of his debilitation.

Jupiter provides good results if placed in houses 1, 5, 8, 9 and 12, but 6th, 7th and the 10th are the bad houses for him.

Just like Sun if Vipreet Rajyoga is formed by Jupiter , it will get support directly or indirectly by all other planets being the teacher of all of them and being the most respectful entity. Jupiter can give it's best Vipreet Rajyoga results for Capricorn Lagna as it is the only Ascendant in which Jupiter is a core Maraka or evil planet by having the lordship of two bad houses 3rd and 12th and that is one of the most important reason why Capricorn is considered as the ascendant of past life sinners because the most benefic became the most malefic for them even worse than Sun the 8th house lord.

Venus – An artist, a lover, a rich man, with divine looks, have all materialistic pleasures like big houses, immense wealth and company of beautiful girls, this is how you can define another teacher Venus.

Venus is also considered as the most benefic planet but off course after Jupiter the only difference is Venus gives success whereas Jupiter gives satisfaction. I know that this concept is hard to understand so I am putting one of my relevant posts from my astrology Facebook page amazing astrology here-

World very often runs on opposite forces
good bad, white black, success and satisfaction, Venus and Jupiter.
You must have seen people around you working on a good post in government or MNC having beautiful wife, obedient children, having a semi luxurious car,3 bedroom flat and very happy in life because he is satisfied with what he has and you must have read or heard about the suicides committed by big superstars and models despite of having lots of sexual relationships, immense wealth and fame have your ever think why?
in our horoscope the karka (cause) of wealth and luck is considered as Jupiter but this is not the whole truth Jupiter is basically karka of your satisfaction in life the lagnas or ascendants ruled by Jupiter or kundalies where Jupiter is yogkarka are the guys of middle or upper middle class like IAS, PCS, Doctors etc. Jupiter is basic karka of satisfaction it can never give you immense wealth and fame until vipreet rajyoga or neechbhanga rajyoga occurs in the lagnas ruled either by Saturn or by Venus.
Venus is the real karka of fame remember moon is considered as karka of fame but that is wrong moon makes person fine artist but there are many fine artists who remain unknown during their lifetime and even if they are known they failed to gain materialistic wealth from their art and fame. Its Venus which gives you fame, luxury and sexual affairs and immortal name if it conjuncts Venus and Jupiter in your kundalii.
But what Venus lacks is satisfaction.
You may ride in Ferrari but you will miss riding on rickshaw

you may have sex with several girls but you will not be able to marry the girl you love.

You may become very famous but you crave for social freedom.

Everything is not meant for everyone.

Some of the unique horoscopes like Mr.Amitabh Bacchan where both Venus and Jupiter are involved in one or both of unorthodox Yogas like Neech bhanga and Vipreet rarely you will see a completely happy person.

Jupiter ruled guys always regret at the later stages of their life that they have wasted their life in family and social circle and Venus ruled person always regret for what they don't have ignoring the wealth and luxuries they already possess.

But one thing is very sure if you really think big in life specially Makar or Capricorn lagna born you must choose Venus as it can give you immortal fame.

Exalted Sun OR Jupiter can hardly makes you an IAS ,PCS but exalted Saturn or Venus can make you whom IAS,PCS serves so if Saturn or Venus is your Yogkaraka always worship them for

Although one of the most benefic planet yet Venus has intrinsic qualities of a demon and Venus is considered as the Teacher of Demons and competitor of Jupiter, one must not get confused between competitor and rival, Venus and Jupiter both are Teachers and their competition involves gaining knowledge and power for themselves rather than hurting others strength that is the reason why their conjunction considered as very beneficial in Kundali.

The Vipreet Rajyogas created by Venus are somewhat similar to Jupiter but the solo difference is that an individual having Vipreet Rajyoga from Venus very often became a person of loose morals and bad habits.

The fame and wealth comes through fashion industry, marriage, love affair, cinema, music, cosmetic industry and other identical sources.

The best thing is the wealth which came will go beyond measurements. The person will live luxurious life with complete materialistic pleasures.

Venus offers very good results if posited in the 2nd, 3rd, 4th, 7th and 12th houses, but the 1st, 6th and 9th houses are considered bad for Venus. It exalted in house 12 and weak in house 6.

Saturn – The Darkness, The fear, limitations, the judge, longevity, struggle this is what Saturn is. A completely evil planet but the best for the creation of Vipreet Rajyoga . The Vipreet Rajyogs where the creator is Saturn generally delivered after the age of 32 years or even late but as Vipreet Rajyogas are connected with evil powers and Saturn is the only non-shadow planet which is considered to be completely evil , it's power is strongest among the all as Vipreet Rajyogas by Saturn gives power along with name, wealth and fame.

A sudden success in politics, business and other authority related fields comes with the blessings of Saturn. When Saturn is the cause behind Vipreet Rajyoga it will get the support of two other completely evil planets. One is the magnifier Rahu (head of the serpent) which enhance the effects of Vipreet Rajyogas and other is the Immense but directionless energy Ketu (tail of the serpent) and if they came into play they can enhance the outcome of Vipreet Rajyoga over 24 times.

The best things in Vipreet Rajyogas created by Saturn are power and longevity, the Vipreet Rajyogas fashioned by Saturn lasts for the lifetime on an individual.

Saturn is measured for good in houses 2nd , 3rd and 7th to 12th, whereas 1st, 4th, 5th and 6th houses are bad for Saturn. Saturn gets exalted in 7th house and the 1st house is the house of its debilitation.

Shadow Planets or Rahu (head of the serpent) and ketu (tail of the serpent) –

So here I am here to discuss about the true nature, qualities and effects of the shadow planets in Vedic astrology called Rahu and Ketu after reading some stupid remarks from some half astrologers like as ketu is the shadow planet of mars so it will also get exalted in Capricorn like mars as it should behave like mars being its shadow.

This was a good joke to refresh your mood but on the serious note I came to know that the level of misconception about shadow planets is so high among people.

Now the first question is

what is a shadow planet and does it really behaves like their original depositors?

A shadow planet is without any mass and yes they behave like their depositors like Rahu the shadow of Saturn and Ketu the Shadow of Mars but behaving like Saturn and mars does not mean that they have qualities and attributes of Mars and Saturn just like your shadow will behave like you if you kick your shadow will also kick, if you sit your shadow will also sit but it doesn't mean that you and your shadow are same.

You may be five feet tall but the length of your shadow depends upon the direction of light it can be ten feet tall or even one feet, in the absence of light your shadow vanishes but you still exists so behaving like someone and having qualities like someone are two very different things.

Now come to Rahu.

Who is Rahu?

In Vedas Rahu is said to be a head but no lower body part, no stomach, no heart etc.

Rahu represents illusion, materialistic desires, greed, fear, black magic. Rahu has a mouth with which it can eat but it can never be satisfied as he has no body to disburse what it eats, it just want more more and more of everything.

For those ignorant person who believe that shadow has the quality of the depositor must know that Rahu is the shadow of Saturn and Saturn denotes limits, boundaries, tradition, contraction whereas Rahu acts as an amplifier it enlarges everything it touches of the sign and house it sits in.

Houses in which Rahu said to give good results are-

1, 3,6,11

Signs suitable for Rahu-

Taurus, Gemini and cancer is Mooltrikona

Exalted in Taurus (It is believed but not proved)

Now ketu, Ketu is a headless body , an extreme energy but without any direction as it has full body but no brain so if it sits with or aspect by strong planet of relevant lagna or ascendant it gives very quick success

Houses good for ketu-

2,9, 10, 11, 12

Signs for ketu-

Exalted in Sagittarius (believed)

Scorpio and Capricorn is its Mooltrikona

But despite of all these things the analysis of Rahu and Ketu is most difficult as for example if Ketu sits in particular lagna say in Capricorn ascendant it us very beneficial as it gives good looks but at the same time gives deceptive personality the nakshatras plays the most vital role in analysis of Rahu and Ketu so the Navmansha chart must be studied carefully and yes never underestimate the power of shadow planets they give the quickest and the biggest success if well poised in your Kundali .

Rahu and Ketu neither can create Rajyogas or Vipreet Rajyogas but yes Rahu can amplify its outcome and Ketu can speed it up.

The most unique and unrevealed secrets about Rahu and Ketu is although they are shadows of Saturn and Mars but they possess qualities of Jupiter. Rahu magnifies as Jupiter does and Ketu gives Moksha or Nirvana which is the biggest quality of Jupiter. Jupiter considered as the Karka or cause of Luck, the game changer in quick succession and Rahu and Ketu are the fastest table turners.

But again the same logic applies here, the body or actions may be of a saint but the soul is of a sinner. Jupiter multiplies the wealth through good means which will benefit others also and Rahu also multiplies the wealth but by wrong means like gambling, lottery etc. because of which wealth comes to an individual at the loss of the others

Ketu give Moksha or Nirvana but Jupiter delivers the same through satisfactory life and happiness but Ketu gives by failures, depression and give up attitude by an individual.

But all in all being core evil forces they are extremely helpful in creating Vipreet Rajyogas and other than their inherent evil nature their rigid placement positions are also very helpful in this.

If Rahu is in Lagna then Ketu will be in the seventh house, ifRahu will be in second then Ketu will be in the eighth house, so Rahu and ketu will be at the difference of seven places from one another.

Now consider these placements –

Rahu in 6th house then Ketu will be in 12th

Rahu in 8th then Ketu will be in 2nd

Rahu in 12th then Ketu will be in 6th

So, such placements will cover evil to evil effect (as Second house is also the place of first Markesh).

And suppose if 6th lord is sitting in 12th house with Rahu and 12th lord is sitting in 6th house with Ketu then a supreme Vipreet Rajyoga will be created but with the support of other planets as both Rahu and Ketu lacks direct action powers.

This theory also applies to Rajyogas where the role of Rahu and Ketu remains the same.

Rahu amplifies and Ketu speed ups.

Rahu gets exalted in houses 3 and 6, whereas he gets debilitated in houses 8, 9 and 11. 12th house is his own house and he proves highly auspicious in houses 3,4 and 6.

6th house is considered to be own house of Ketu. It gives its exalted effect when in 5th, 9th or 12th house and its debilitated effect in 6th and 8th house. Day is its time and it represents Sunday as day.

True Nature and communities of Planets –

Deva Planets or Divine Planets – They may signify anger, cruelty or love but the integral nature will be divine only they are as follows -

- Sun – The natural atmkaraka or the creator of soul

- Moon – The signifier of Mind

- Mars – Indicates tangible body

- Jupiter – The divine Knowledge

Demon Planets or Evil planets – Their outcome may be beneficial but their true nature will be demonic they are as follows –

- Venus – The materialistic wealth governed by Venus the root cause of all the evil in this world.

- Saturn – The creator of Darkness

- Rahu – Fear and Greed gives money but through bad sources

- Ketu - Gives Moksha but only after continuous failures and depression in life.

Mercury is the balancing factor it absorbs the effects of the houses or zodiac signs in which it sits

Vrana or Class of planets –

I often see less knowledge guys to blame that Hinduism is based on jaati vyavastha or cast system rather than Hinduism is based on Varna Vyavastha or the Class system the first system of specialization on earth in which a certain community is specialized in doing a particular kind of work so just like humans our holy Rishis (Saga) allotted class to planets they are as below –

- Bramhin – The planets belong to this class are teachers and mostly benefic whether they produce benefits through right way or wrong way, they are specially beneficial in Rajyogas and for Vipreet Rajyogas they should be at their most evil points.

There are three planets in this category – Jupiter, Venus and Ketu and among these three Ketu is most beneficial for Vipreet Rajyoga as it is a naturally evil planet.

- Kshatriya – The planets falls into this category are warriors and have equal strength in creating Rajyogas and Vipreet Rajyogas depending upon the level of evilness they hold in Kundali or birth charts.

Two planets belongs to this group – Sun and Mars

- Shudra – Planets which are Shudra class are very hard working and beneficial for Vipreet Rajyogas as they are related with illusion and materialistic wealth rather than Nirvana or Divine Knowledge.

Saturn and Rahu belong to this category.

- Vaishya – This is the class for businessmen, the versatility, adaptation to alien conditions, skill of mind. Mercury belong to this class and it is exceptionally mysterious planet good for nothing and good for everything at the same time so it is effected mostly by the placements of other planets.

Measurements of the strength and weakness of the planets –

Strength and weakness of planets are the only criteria on which the outcome depends and that depends upon the following conditions –

- Placements of planets

- Degree wise strength of planets

- Favorable Conjunctions or Yogas

- Raj Yogas

- Vipreet Rajyogas

- Neech Bhanga Rajyogas

Placements of Planets –

Placements Of planets have two classifications –

1. Based on Bhavas or Houses

2. Based on Zodiac Signs

Based on signs – Signs holds more importance than houses as they drives out the open energy, anyways they required the under support of the houses but yet signs define 60% of the planet's strength.

The signs classification are-

- Exalted or Uccha – It is considered to be the best placement for any planet. Exalted house is the house of full freedom for any planet and it is also considered as better placement then the Mooltrikona or own house.

  For example – If you goes to your best friend's house you will have more freedom than into your own house as you will be free from any proxy or supervision.

  The planet which is exalted gives beneficial outcomes to an individual throughout his/her lifetime but on the houses where their malefic aspect falls the benefits eroded.

  For example – In Aries ascendant Saturn gets exalted in Libra in the seventh house so it will increase the beneficial results of tenth and eleventh house as he owns then, the best results will came from seventh house but due to his malefic aspect on first house or ascendant he will deprive an individual from good looks,increase depression, put him into the legal issues etc.

When lord of the evil houses gets exalted they continue to give bad effects but the best effect related to the house which they have lordship will come.

For example if Saturn owns eighth house and gets exalted, it will give troubles but ensure longevity of life and delayed but desired success.

- Mooltrikona or Self Zodiac Sign – When a planet comes into the zodiac sign which is owned and controlled by him shows very good results, It is like being into your own home, the master, all in all everything.

  But unlike Exalted planet a planet in its Mooltrikona gives favorable results only during the times of its own major periods, sub periods and minor periods.

  When an evil house lord comes into its Mooltrikona then it is the best placement for it, I am getting off beat from traditional astrological view because if one evil house lord goes into another evil house it will destroy evil effects of that particular house. For example if the 6th house lord goes into the 8th house it will minimize the ups and downs of the life and provide him with wealth. By doing this it is providing him the indirect benefit.

  If a planet comes into his Mooltrikona it is like no matter how bad you are , you will never destroy your own house, you will keep your house clean and hence will give the direct benefits.

  Say if Sun is the 8th lord and goes into the eight house then person will have magnetic effect in his surroundings, he will be long lived; he will be able to keep the secrets and drive benefits out of them.

Although its aspects **will** again be mostly malefic but for its own house it will be good.

- Friendly Zodiac – This is a little confusing position as it can be good or sometimes very good. Depends upon the position of the friendly planet in Kundali or birth charts.

  For example – For Capricorn ascendant Saturn is placed in friendly sign of Virgo in the house of luck the 9th house and its owner Mercury gets exalted then in this position Saturn can give better than its best as it will get the support of its friend Mercury which also holds the house of luck.

- Weak or Neech Sign – These are the signs in which planets have minimum potential of giving any positive outcome. Neither freedom of movement nor the exhale of energy is available their but with Vipreet Rajyoga or NeechBhanga Rajyoga this position can be very beneficial.

  Yet for the houses on which their beneficial aspect falls they give good results.

- Enemy Sign – This is the worst sign as the planets which falls in its enemy sign gives adverse results but on contrary this position is best for Vipreet Rajyogas.

The table of Exaltation, Self Zodiac or Mooltrikona, Friendly, weak and enemy signs is given below –

Planets	Zodia Lordship	Exalted Sign	Weak Sign	Friendly Sign	Enemy Sign

Sun	Leo	Aries	Libra	Cancer, Scorpio, Sagittarius, Pisces	Virgo, Libra, Aquarius
Moon	Cancer	Taurus	Scorpio	Virgo, Gemini, Leo	None
Mars	Aries, Scorpio	Capricorn	Cancer	Sagittarius, Pisces, Leo	Gemini ,Virgo
Mercury	Gemini, Virgo	Virgo	Pisces	Taurus, Leo, Leo	None
Jupiter	Sagittarius, Pisces	Cancer	Capricorn	Aries,Leo, Cancer, Scorpio	Virgo, Gemini, Libra, Taurus
Venus	Taurus, Libra	Pisces	Virgo	Gemini, Virgo, Capricorn, Aquarius	Aries,Cancer, Leo,Scorpio
Saturn	Capricorn, Aquarius	Libra	Aries	Gemini ,Virgo, Taurus	Cancer, Leo, Scorpio
Rahu	None	Taurus, Gemini	Scorpio, Sagittarius	Virgo, Libra	None
Ketu	None	Scorpio, Sagittarius	Taurus, Gemini	None	None

Note –Astrology learners more often than not raised the questions like
why Mars gets exalted in its arch enemy's house the house of Saturn or

Why Venus gets exalted in the sign of Jupiter the rival of Venus? Why Mars gets exalted in Capricorn and not in Aquarius which is also owned by Saturn? Why Venus doesn't exalted in Sagittarius because just like Pisces Jupiter owns Sagittarius also?

The answer is pretty complex but very logical. For instance why Sachin Tendulkar's performance was best against Australia whereas his performance was average against few comparatively weak teams? Why Rahul Dravid performed his best in the alien conditions and on the toughest grounds rather than his own home grounds or friendly Asian sub-continent grounds?

First of all you must understand the differences in between the Zodiac Signs and their relationships with their lords.

Aquarius or Kummbha is the Mooltrikona or self-sign of Saturn and a less known fact is this that it is also Punya Rashi (Divine Zodiac Sign) of Saturn whereas Capricorn is the Paap Rashi (Sinner Zodiac Sign) of Saturn.

Look it from this prospective suppose you own two houses one is your favorite where you love to live with your family and other you keep your unwanted guests in sort of a trial room or test zone. Capricorn is a test zone created by Saturn and the guys who born in Capricorn Lagna or ascendant are past life sinners.

The lagna or ascendant of Sinners, the lagna with maximum effect of demonic powers and malefic effects from the divine, the lagna of those who had committed serious sins in their past lives like demolishing any religious place, killing priests or religious animals etc. It's Capricorn.
The unique observations about Capricorn are-
Liars, tendency of secret revenge, hard to judge, natural deceivers, early success almost impossible.
Saturn denotes darkness whereas Mars signifies fire the light, Saturn denotes stillness and Mars denotes speed, action ,courage, Saturn is the sign of old age and Mars of vigilant youth so all in all its opposite

attracts theory coupled with a very important fact that Mars is also a cruel and partially evil planet and for Capricorn ascendant it owns 4th and 11th house.

Jupiter which is the most beneficial planet becomes the real punisher in the evil sign of Saturn. The best delivers its worst.

But sinners also have two classifications – A sinner by will and a sinner by mistake. The guys who have done some bad deeds by mistake gets exalted Mars to gain that violent force and courage to contradict the challenges.

Now about Venus why it gets exalted in Pisces, see there is a healthy competition in between Jupiter and Venus, jealousy, hate is their but the mode is very different, say there are two brilliant students in a class and both are competing with each other but their competition will be healthy, they both have their own notes, study materials and some secret ways to study.

Suppose one student who is a little stealthy nature gets the access into the study room of another than what will happen? He will get unauthorized access to his study material and he will improve his performance to the utmost. Venus is a demon teacher and even after being a teacher the demonic tendencies are there, it is a materialistic planet and of loose morals. So Venus in Pisces is Venus getting access to Jupiter's divine knowledge and resources and all in all excels its performance.

On the contrary Jupiter will never do this as a planet of divine pride and rules.

The same idea governs the fact that conjunction of Jupiter and Venus is always beneficial because of healthy competition among them, they improve their performance for being on ladder's top. So, knowing the true nature of the houses and zodiac signs is very essential.

The dual sign ownership is like owing two houses or owing two room house where one is your bedroom and other is guest room, you will not allow your guests to come into your bedroom, it doesn't mean that they are your enemies but their relationship with you is not very close.

- Degree wise strength – Some guys complain that even if they have good placements in their Kundali they are not getting beneficial results why?

The answer is quite a bit simple. Suppose you have an exalted Mars in Capricorn of 5 degrees but yet you are struggling is just like you have hire a warrior but his age is just 6 years. So having Degree wise strength is as important as house and zodiac sign strength.

Every planet hold its position from 0 - 30 degrees in sky and the degree wise strength is the most vital factor for giving the final outcome. Consider one of your friend is very keen to help you but he himself is weak so how will he help you out or your Venus is exalted in Birth Kundali but the only of 2 degrees so how will he give you money when he himself lacks it or your enemy wants to hurt you but he lacks power , say Marak (evil) planet is sitting with 4 degrees will not be able to harm you so in both cases they are not been able to do anything.

The degree wise subdivision is as given below -

00 degree - A new born child totally helpless have no importance. If your evil planets like mars if you are manglik or markesh (most evil planets) is at this degree than you are lucky the evil effects will be subsided.

0- 6 degrees -Weak planets hardly give 10% of the results either good or bad for example if your placement of planets signify 100 rupee of gain you will get only rupee 10 and in case of 100 rupee deficit it will result in only 10 rupee away from you.

0 degree – No importance

6- 12 - degree - 50% of results.

12- 18 degree - purna yuva or complete youth provide 100% of results.

18- 24- Mid aged provide 50% of results

24- 30- 10% of results

30 degree - no importance

House or Bhavas vs Zodiac Signs – The answer is preety simple for delivering the full effect both are required. The houses holds the $1/4^{th}$ value of outcome and rest $3/4^{th}$ is hold by the singn in which the planet is sitting, obviously signs has more value but to reap out the full benefits both houses and signs are required.

- Favorable Conjunctions or Yogas –

There are verities of Yogas in Vedic astrology but most important are Mahabhagya Yogas, Panch Mahapurush Yogas and many others.

- Raj Yogas (Kingly conjunctions) – You cannot describe darkness without light, Sadness without Happiness and Paucity without abundance so for explaining Vipreet Rajyogas or NeechBhanga Rajyogas first we will have to understand what RajYogas are.

  It is impossible to make someone understand the hundreds and thousands kinds of RajYogas defined by our divine Rishis (Saga) but I am trying my level best to provide my readers the best possible explanation.

  So the cardinal requirements of RajYogas to deliver their full results are as follows –

  1. Lord of ascendant or Lagnesh, Yogkaraka (Most active planet of Kundali and Navmesh (Lord of the ninth house is in between 12 to 18 degrees.

  2. All the planets are in between 12 to 18 degrees

  3. Quadrant or Trine has more than three planets

4. More than two planets will be in Exaltation signs or Mooltrikona (self signs).

5. If four or more planets are in friendly signs

6. Exchange of houses in between Trine and Quadrant lords.

7. If four or more than four planets in quadrants

8. Aspect or conjunction in between the Trine and Quadrant lord

9. Connection by aspect, houses or exchange in between the trine and Quadrant lords from the moon

10. Trine lords or Quadrant lords in their own signs or Mooltrinkona

11. Lagna Lord well placed in trine.

So above is a very brief explanation of RajYogas obviously there are many more and as this book is on off beat RajYogas so only brief knowledge is given. RajYogas are very favorable, timely and satisfaction providing combination but it doesn't denotes Kingship rather it indicates headship.

If you are working as a branch executive in a company you will become branch manager during your RajYoga time period. If you are a care taker of a building you will become an owner of that building during your RajYoga period.

Rajyogas generally give outcomes based on the family backgrounds, social status and personal traits. For example - Son of a doctor becomes doctor, son of an IAS become IAS , it also give rise to an individual but only up to certain level like a son of a doctor becomes much more famous and rich than his father and same level.

Vipreet Rajyoga – As the name suggests Vipreet (opposite) Rajyoga

(Kingly combination) or the placements of the planets in the signs and houses in a particular Kundali which will be exactly opposite to Rajyogas, the benefits comes from the Vipreet Rajyogas are hundreds and thousands time more than the present social status and family background of a person but in adverse circumstances or by the loss of the others.

Vipreet Rajyoga can make beggar a king, a normal person a celebrity, a soldier a king and so on and if it is coupled with Neech Bhanga Rajyoga (cancellation of weakness) then it will be more powerful than thousands of Rajyogas.

Major conditions under which Vipreet Rajyogas are created are mentioned below –

- 6th lord in 8th or 12th house,8th lord in 6th or 12th house and 12th lord in 6th or 8th house this is best of the best Vipreet Rajyoga

- If two or more than two planets are in their weak or enemy sign placed in 6th ,8th or 12th houses.

- Four or more than four planets are placed in 3rd .6th ,8th,11th or in 12th houses in their weak or enemy sign.

- LordS OF THE Quadrant or Trine are in their exaltation signs in 3rd ,6th ,8th ,11th or 12th house.

- If three or more than three planets are placed in 6th ,8th or 12th house with one evil house lord but there should be no benefic planet

- If an evil house lord is in its Mooltrikona in 6th ,8th or 12th house

- Two or more evil house owners are placed in an evil house together.

- If in all quadrants there are evil planets and in evil houses benefic planets.

- All planets come to one side of Rahu and Ketu (It is also called Kaal Sarpa yoga and under some circumstances it creates extremely strong Vipreet Rajyoga).

- 6th, 8th, 12th or 3rd house lords in their sign of exaltation in quadrants or trine.

- All the planets sits under the degree of 5 or over 25 in Kundali or birth charts.

So there will be Vireet Rajyogas in the above mentioned conditions few more conditions are also there related to 2nd house and 7th house and Navmansha which will be explained in the proceeding chapters of this book with examples.

The intensity of Vipreet Rajyogas on the house wise is as follows

- 6th ,8th and 12th houses are worst houses

- 3rd and 11th house partially evil

- 2nd and 7th house conditionally evil

Differences between RajYogas and Vipreet Rajyogas

Raj Yogas	Vipreet Rajyogas
Form due to the connection in between Quadrants and Trine lords	For due to the connection in between evil house lords
Rajyogas created by good or divine planets then person will get the desired success easily	If Vipreet Rajyoga created by Good planets one has to struggle for his achievements
When evil planets create this yoga one has to struggle for his	When evil planets create this yoga

success	success comes all of a sudden
The results deliver timely	Results come suddenly but generally in later stages of life
The level of life gets up to considerable level when these Yogas occurs	The level of life became exceptionally high
An individual with this yoga person lives happy and satisfactory life and his influence will be in his community and family	An individual will live life of struggle and hard work but his name and fame will be all across the world and in later stages of life he will live like a king
After the death his name vanishes with passage of time	His name will be immortal

The real outcome of success or failure, satisfaction and achievement can be analyzed with the combination of Rajyogas and Vipreet Rajyogas in a particular kundali or birth charts.

The exceptional points in Vipreet Rjyogas are –

1. A person on having Rajyoga becomes a millionaire by his hard work and skills whereas on having Vipreet Rajyoga he becomes millionaire overnight by winning a lottery, getting hidden wealth, casino or any other such sources.

2. One person becomes Member of Parliament because of his family background and another person becomes Prime Minister although belong to an unknown family background.

3. One person devotes his whole life in getting scared divine powers through Yogas and tantra and another person found it without any efforts.

4. So conclusion is Vipreet Rajyoga is outcome of past life deeds or Karmas

Vipreet means opposite the person who behaves contrary or opposite to his cast, community, culture or situation in his past life very often born with this yoga.

Just like a cow recognizes her calf among the thousands of calves our Karmas or deeds recognizes us in thousands of lives and births I will explain this in my upcoming books for now read these examples –

Suppose you are very hungry and you have only one bread to eat and you see a hungry old man in front of you then what will you do?

Under the normal circumstances you will ignore him and eat the full bread and under the liberal circumstances you will share your bread with him but under extremely divine situation you will react completely opposite to the situation and feed him up keeping yourself hungry.

For first situation you will get adverse yogas in next life

For second situation you qualify for RajYogas

For third situation you will be a qualified person for Vipreet Rajyoga.

In our puranas also there is a Tale let me narrate that –

During the time of Mahabharata when King Yudhisthir was performing RajSurya yagya (most divine worship in Hinduism) ,King Yudhisthir becomes disdainful because of the huge donations he had given during this process and one day he asked Lord Shree Krishna that is there is anyone more charitable than me then Lord Shree Krishna smiled and said you will get the answer after the sunset today.

On that Sunset there comes a jackle and his half body was of gold so king Yudhisthir wondered and asked the jackle the secret behind this so the jackle unrevealed his tale he said –

O great King, I had been very hungry last night and visited an old temple in the nearby forest inhabited by a bheel (people who live in jungle) family consist of a couple and two kids a girl and a boy, they had been starving from last three days and today by the grace of God they had got four chapatis (Indian bread) to eat which was not even suitable to sustain the complete diet of this family but they had given me their share of food one by one to feed me completely and they themselves starved to death and when I came out from that place my half body turned into gold.

That Bheel and his family had reborn for next 21 lives as King of the kings because of acting completely opposite to the natural circumstances.

Now for another example – If one is born in a charitable and rich family and get accustomed with good culture and customs and he too becomes a good man in life then it will be normal. But if boy who is a son of a bandit and groom up among the bandits and greedy people and if he becomes good person and a kind hearted individual the he is acting opposite to his natural custom and society as a result in his next life after the struggles to foot up for his past life sins he will get grand life as a result of his offbeat behavior of kindness.

So God is never unfair to anyone we get what we deserve Raj Yogas or Vipreet Rajyogas all are outcome of our actions.

This is the only reason why that the evil house lords and natural karkas acts against their core nature and makes the person a king.

A coward person sacrificed his life for his nation acting against his own nature will get a Vipreet Rajyoga created by Mars in next life so this is the core explanation of Vipreet Rajyoga's causes now we will have to move ahead.

Major house Vipreet Rajyogas in general –

6th house – Owned by Mercury and Natural Karka is Ketu. Mercury is identity less planet so as Ketu the tail of a serpent has full body but not head, no identity, no direction. So sixth house is for diseases, enemies, debts etc. but from unwanted and unknown sources.

You can take loan from your very good friend then what? You will have flexibility in repayment but what if you took loan from a greedy person? He will take no mercy on you. So, debts in 6th house denotes to tough positions, unwanted enemies, unpleasant situations.

But one thing one should always remember both Mercury and Ketu are exceptional planets, Mercury the faceless messenger which can incarnate into any planet and other is Ketu which can speed up even a mountain.

- Ketu if sits in 6th house it always destroys enemies and diseases.

- Guru no matter whichever house or zodiac sign it owe it always remove diseases from the life of an individual if sits in 6th house.

- If Ketu sits with any planet in its Mooltrikona it speeds up its effect twice and increase its outcome four times whether good or bad.

- 6th lord in 6th house – No enemies, no diseases, no debts even if debt or enemies will get removed soon. The planet sits in 6th house aspects 12th house so will also get relief from the troubles from the 12th house.

- 6th lord in 8th house – A person can be a great doctor or a healer, an individual will be long lived with good health and travel to overseas land, and he will gain fixed assets in life.

- 6th lord in 12th house – Life will be full of adversities but every adversity will turn out to be an opportunity after a long struggle, get sick only in the last phase of life, will get support from maternal uncle. Such an individual gain great name and wealth but after a great struggle and put among the great personalities by the general masses. He will be real table turner and many times it looks life that his life is finished and he is defeated but all of the sudden he changes the complexion of the picture of life in his favor. A real champion is born if 12th house has got no aspect from any benefic planet.

The other Vipreet Rajyogas with low intensity are when 6th lord is in other evil houses then even he will be gaining support even from their enemies and fulfilling of worldly desires.

- 8th house – The worst house.

- Eighth house Curse or Blessing in Disguise
- "Some changes look negative on the surface,
  But you will soon realize that space is being created in your life
  For something new to emerge."
  I have heard enough negative conclusions now about the
  Randra bhava or the eighth house as well as the eighth lord as it
  is the house of death and the lord governs your life span.
  But one thing which everyone forgets that there is a unique
  concept of death in Vedas it never takes the conclusion of death
  as an end but as a complete change.
  The reality is this that after trine houses it is only house eighth
  which can give sudden and grand success to an individual as
  eighth house is the house of sudden wealth, secrecy and the
  ultimate price which we will pay in our life for success.
  If eighth lord is exalted two things becomes sure first there will
  be great hurdles to the success of an individual and other he will
  cross every hurdle although it will take a bit long time but no
  worries as it also confirms the purna ayu yoga or long life.
  If eighth lord comes into its own sign or Mooltrikona then the
  person will be trustworthy and he will again get long life but
  numerous ups and downs in life but no matter how much down
  he falls he will surely make a sudden come back a bit surprising
  changes in life which seems to be negative in the beginning but
  ends up with positivity in life.

If your eighth lord is in 6th or 12th house or under some conditions in 2nd or 7th or 11th houses it can give rise to Vipreet Rajyoga

If you eighth lord conjuncts 6th or 12th lord it assure your success in life sooner or later and if your lagna lord is strong then larger than expected success is in wait for you.

The eighth house is considered to be the most strong point for Vipreet Raj Yoga as it is the worst house in any Kundali but as per my perception the guys with strong eighth house gets immortal fame and money in offbeat and innovative fields.

- It is ruled by Mars and Natural Karka is both Mars and Saturn the arch enemies but one of the biggest astrology secrets is this the conditional ties among these two planets.

Take an example suppose the owner or the caption of Indian cricket team Mr.M.S.Dhoni and the best player of Indian team Virat Kohli hold bad blood with each other and try to harm each other's reputation directly or indirectly but when India goes into world cup all of a sudden they leave their personal traits and started playing for the pride of their nation and try to give their best as this condition demands their commitment so same is here with the Vipreet Rajyogas created in eighth house.

- 8th lord in the 6th house – The person will be the owner of the hidden wealth or get wealth from completely unknown and unaware sources. Wealth can be in form of money, assets or secret paranormal powers as eighth house rules super human entities also. 8th house is 11th to 6th house which means partial evil and partial enemy with benefits so this individual is completely apt in making his enemies his friends. He rarely gets sick.

If the eighth house lord is a naturally benefic planet then individual gets name d fame through politics or social service and goes overseas for many times. If lord of the eighth house is an evil planet then the results will be magnifies several times, he will gain everything in life on his own efforts and his fame will become immortal.

- If lord of the eighth house is in the eighth house so an individual is an innovator of a completely new ideology or thinking which will continue to inspire the several generations even after him.

The ideology can be scientific or super normal like astrology, black magic, mythological or any other. These individuals are gifted with the spiritual knowledge by birth, although they will be under mental tension for long period of life and even after continuous struggle he is always lucky to gain more than the expected fruits of his efforts.

Not only his present birth but even his coming rebirths will carry his intelligence. After a long struggle and problems his identity will be completely changes but changes for good.

- Eighth lord in the 12th house – 12th house ruled by Jupiter and Natural Karka is Rahu.One is most divine planet and other is most evil. But Jupiter is very powerful planet but yet Rahu is the fastest so it puts several hurdles in the ways.

    Jupiter signifies divine knowledge and Rahu an illusion, Jupiter leads to Nirvana or Moksha but Rahu indicates materialistic greed. Eighth lord in the twelfth house signifies hardest troubles in life but after an age long struggle and fight an individual gets immortal fame and became role model for entire nation.

    A trailblazer to a great achievements but mostly they get major share of fame after their life so somehow a very harsh yoga as the receiver of this yoga enjoys only a little benefit during his lifetime.

    Other Vipreet Rajyogas for 8th lord in general –

- 8th lord in 2nd house – Second house owner is Venus whereas Natural Karka is Jupiter the rivals but not enemies and if 8th lord sits in second house it aspects his own house that means 8th house and the biggest advantage of this position is the person has got all the probabilities to be very rich in life as second house also denotes to wealth. No wonder with such placement if a person becomes a dollar making machine from a penny less beggar.

The person will be a creator of such a technology or theory which will bring about a complete change in the relevant industry as 8th house also represents rebirth or change of personality or identity.

- Eighth lord in third house – It is very auspicious as 3rd house is 8th house from eighth house itself so it becomes super evil naturally. It creates superb Vipreet Rajyoga. A real warrior born with such placement, always dare to challenge death and defy it successfully. A one man team, a one man army if aspect by other malefic or evil planets. Gains wealth from all possible sources but if the creator of Vipreet Rajyoga is an evil planet and conjunct with Rahu or Ketu than individual can be in the crime world but yet living with rule and dignity.

- Eighth Lord in Eleventh house – The person will be of very sharp wit as this house is ruled by Saturn and the natural Karka are both Saturn and Jupiter. The person will be magnetic, sharp minded, they gain much more money in accordance to the effort they put in to. Sudden and big gain of money is also very much probable.

They can be politicians, mass media person and businessman also.

- • Twelfth house –The final outcome of the life, the end result, the summery of achievements and failures. It is ruled by the most divine planet Jupiter and Natural karka is most malefic planet the Rahu but both are the magnifiers so here are the Vipreet Rajyogas for 12th house in general –

- Twelfth lord in sixth house – Absence of enemies and diseases even of they happen to be they will be removed without any personal efforts. The best part is these guys are bound to be very good investors as twelfth lord is the lord of expenses and from sixth house it aspect its own house so they recover expenses very well in short they will definitely earn more than their investments.

Usually these guys first earn money and then name through that money by putting it into society welfare, these guys are employment generators and earn money and name cross borders and worshiped in true senses by the society. Their maternal uncles and aunties also support them well and prove to be lucky for them.

- In eighth house the twelfth lord – In the worst house a saint cames, twelth house lord in the eighth house fulfills the individual's life with enemies and controversies but the person will overcome all of them with his innovative ideology and unexpected supports at the time of need and gets permanent wealth and fame but yet live like a saint, travel overseas also and be of a very good character.

- 12th lord in the 12th house – Best position as these guys gets whatever they want but very late in life, they will be long lived and best of the best knowledgeable person, very rude and angry by nature from outside but very merciful at heart. If Rahu joins the twelfth lord in twelfth house the results will come little quicker before middle age.

  The other Vipreet Rajyogas are –

- 12th lord in second house – If of a weak or enemy sign will increase wealth from abroad.

- 12th lord in third house – Very brave, displays exceptional valor at international level and gain money and name at international level.

- 12th lord in the 11th house – The person will gain fortune far away from his birth place. He will struggle till he lives in his birth place. Eleventh house is twelfth from twelfth so becomes much more malefic if 12th lord sits in there. Person can be the owner owner of many sources of income and will gain name in his birth place in the later stages of his life

Points of concern –

1. If Vipreet Rajyogas created by naturally benefic or divine planets then their effect will be low. If created in divine zodiac sign the also their effect will be not as expected. Under these conditions the Vipreet Rajyoga will come through regular route and their effects will be good but not grand whereas if Vipreet Rajyoga is created by naturally cruel or evil planets and in evil signs or Lagnas or ascendants the results will be grand and innovative. The fame level will be high.

2. If Rahu or Ketu sits with Vipreet Rajyoga planets they will get the benefit much quickly and the enhanced. If Vipreet Rajyoga planet is in its mooltrikona or own house and ketu is with them the effect will be several times high. Same happens if Jupiter is with them but only if Jupiter is naturally malefic for that particular ascendant and sit in its weak or enemy sign.

3. If the Vipreet Rajyoga planet aspect evil or bad houses the results will be amplified and if they aspect trine or quadrant the effects will be lowered.

For example if Saturn is the lord of twelfth house and sits in sixth house then their will be the following results –

- Third aspect will be on eighth house the worst house

- Seventh aspect on his own house 12th house evil house

- Tenth aspect on the third house bad house of charts in astrology analysis

Therefore such Vipreet Rajyoga will be grand one and if any other evil planet like Rahu or Ketu also occupies one of these houses then the results will be exceptional.

And now substitute the planet Saturn with Mars which is also a naturally cruel planet and sits in the twelfth house then these followings will be the results –

- Fourth aspect will be on third house a bad house.

- Seventh aspect will be on sixth house an evil house

- Eighth aspect will be on 7th house naturally good house

So Vipreet Rajyoga will be only 60% delivered.

Suppose Mars goes into sixth house then it will aspect

- Ninth house the strongest trine in birth chart

- Twelfth house an evil house

- Lagna or ascendant the most important house

The Vipreet Rajyoga will only be 40% fruitful in such case.

So for different ascendants or lagnas and zodiac signs and planets the analysis of Vipreet Rajyoga will be different.

4. If there will be exchange of two or more than two evil houses lord then the Vipreet Rajyoga will be very strong. For instance in Capricorn ascendant Sun the owner of the eighth house and Mercury the owner of sixth house exchange their houses.

5. If there will be exchange of signs in between two or more than two evil house lords in evil houses such Vipreet Rajyoga is excellent.

6. The planets which are evil or cruel are more auspicious for Vipreet Rajyoga like Mars, Saturn and Sun then Vipreet Rajyoga will be more strong and if divine planets creates it then this yoga will be good but not grand enough.

7. Aspect from the evil planet also nourishes Vipreet Rajyoga and aspects from benific planets produce debilitating results.

8. It is very strange that an individual dosent recive the major benefit of Vipreet Rajyoga during the Mahadasha (major period) of the planets which create Vipreet Rajyoga rather they recive this sudden benefit during the Anterdashas (Sub Periods) and Pratyanterdashas (Minor Period).

9. If the planets creating Vipreet Rajyoga are two,three four ,five or even more sits in naturally evil of bad houses exactly in third house, sixth house ,eighth house or in twelfth house under such condition second house got the tendencies of Vipreet Rajyoga automatically (as it is

first markesh and house of liquid money) and under some very scared conditions seventh house also.

10. If second house has two or more than two planets in its enemy or weak sign or an evil planet under such condition also Vipreet Rajyoga created in the second house as planets sits in second house will aspect eighth house and second house is eight from ninth house the house of luck. The more the planets will be in neech or weak sign or in enemy sign and if planet will be evil or cruel person will get that much fame and money all over the world but if divine planets like Venus or Jupiter will be there they will get good money and fame but after long struggle.

11. If in many planets moon also get included then there will be controversy. To be more specific under such condition there will be both Rajyogas and Vipreet Rajyogas at the same time so the person will see its downfall to the deepest and his promotion to the apex in the same life time. But such situation will make an individual's fame everlasting like Hitler or Osho who are studied even after their mortal lives some guys respevt them others hate them.

12. Note under the dual ownership of planet (When one planet owns two signs), the other aspects will come into play. For example Mars owns ascendant and eighth house for Aries Ascendants so for Vipreet Rajyoga he should be in his enemy or weak sign or for Capricorn Mercury owns ninth and sixth house so if he will be in an evil house with cruel or evil planet he will behave like evil planet and if with divine or good planets he will consider as good planet and so on.

Vipreet Rajyoga created by many planets –

As I have already explained the when in one or more than one of the third, sixth ,eighth and twelfth houses Vipreet Rajyoga is created by many planets then the person will be National, social, economic, religious, spiritual or political innovator and established himself as a power and personality that lasts for centuries. It is a general observation that such Vipreet Rajyogas are delivered in the mid age of an individual swing of fortune comes in their favor and they gain wealth and fame globally and their name even after them.

Lagna or Ascendant wise details of Vipreet Rajyoga –

Aries – This is an ascendant of warriors, braves and truthful person but sometimes very rigid. Being a Divine Lagna very useful for RajYogas and Punch Mahapurush Yoga but under very limited circumstances gives strong Vipreet Rajyoga.

Aries means the one who arrives first and fastest, it is very good sign for fighters.

Nine Planets for Aries ascendants –

- Sun – owns 5th house. Best friend of Mars the lagna lord. It governs Consciousness of the existence of Heavenly Acumen, good at speculation, children and other acts of imaginative genius, political power and personality recognition.

1. Sun rules the 5th house a trine and is a associate of Mars.

2. Groups of this ascendant will profit considerably by wearing a Ruby IF Sun need more power.

3. The positive effects of the ruby will be more noticeable in the major period of Sun."

- Moon – Lords over fourth house again a good friend of Mars but the natural attributes are different as moon is a water planet and Mars is fiery. It effects early childhood, attachment to the land and customs of one's people (especially the maternal culture), public tie ups, social obligations.

  1. Moon is the lord of the 4th house a quadrant
  2. The lord of the Ascendant Mars is a friend of Moon.
  3. So by wearing a Pearl one can get good results if moon is benefic and need more power.

- Mars – Lord or ascendant and eighth house.
- Mercury – Owner of the third and sixth house.

- Jupiter – Ninth & twelfth house
- Venus – second and seventh house
- Saturn – Tenth and eleventh house
- Rahu – Partial Lord of 11th house
- Ketu – Partial lord of 8th house

Planets create Vipreet Rajyoga –

- Mercury – Owner of third and sixth house so very malefic planet in normal circumstances but very beneficial when creates Vipreet RajYoga.

- Mars – Lord of the ascendant and owner of eighth house so can deliver average results in Vipreet Rajyoga unless gets into evil, weak or enemy sign or get support from Ketu.

- Saturn – Owner of the tenth house and eleventh house so hardly own any malefic lordship but being a naturally evil planet and arch enemy of Mars in case of Vipreet RajYoga it deliver good results but with considerable delay. If Rahu aspects or sits in 11th house the desires will be fulfilled early.

- Jupiter – Owner of the Ninth house and twelfth house and also a naturally benefic planet so in case of Vipreet RajYoga it will give average results.

Vipreet Rajyoga in various houses for Aries Ascendant or Lagna –

1. Vipreet RajYoga in Third house –

1. If Mercury alone sits in the third house then the person will have many brothers and all will support him, he will be a writer, editor or poet or somehow related to the field of writing if Sun conjuncts Mercury or Buddha Aditya Yoga (when Sun and Mercury sits together) forms in this house the fame will be in many nations. Individual will be lover of games but progress will come easily in the field of writing.

2. If Mars sits in the third house person will be brave and gain name in police and army and will not have elder brothers. He will be rich and his good effects will goes on to next generation.

3. If Saturn sits into the third house the person will have friends and well-wishers in large numbers, person will be long lived, industrialists or big businessman and his business will be in diversified fields. He will gain money and fame after the mid age and his glory will cross the borders but the only loophole is there will be paucity of children or will lack male child and even if he have male child then his child will be non-talented.

4. If Jupiter is in the third house then person will earn more money in comparison to the hard work he applies. He will enjoy family life, goes to religious voyages and will be famous in forging lands; longevity will be an essential outcome.

5. Mercury and Mars together makes a person famous critic or audition in the writing field or if in government sector then will earn more name because of his writing.

6. Mercury and Saturn in this house says that person will be a philosopher and in his early life normal public, friends and even his relatives and family will consider him a fool and day dreamer but in between the age of 35-40 he will gain sudden swing and he will gain great wealth and his thoughts will get popular all across the globe although his education will face many hurdles and it is possible that his education will be incomplete.

7. If Mars and Saturn gets together a real dare devil will born for sure. He will have number of enemies and they will plan many ploys against him but he will overcome all and very often in life gain money and fame by defeating his enemies, they can be businessman, players or politicians, in police department also .

8. If Mars and Jupiter comes together than the person is born lucky guy and will get his share of good luck in between 25-35

years of his age. He shows courage for his country, society, religion and followers and becomes famous and very rich. His family also remains safe during his life.

9. When Mercury and Jupiter sits together than this Vipreet Rajyoga needs support of some other benefic planets also like Venus or other, person will be head of large family and his earning sources will increase with the passage of time, daughters will be lucky for his family and he will enjoy long life although may get diseases in the later stages of life.

10. If there will be three or more planets in the third house then irrespective of their ownership of houses in birth chart strong Vipreet Rajyoga will be formed as Mercury incarnates the effects of more than few planets, generally such guys get popular very early from 15-25 years of their age and gain wealth easily and this happens all of a sudden. If benefic planets are involved then the person will get fame and money because of constructive works and if evil planets are involved then the fame and wealth will be due to controversial of bad ways.

2. Vipreet Rajyogas in the sixth house for Aries Lagna or ascendants –

   1. The person with Mercury in sixth house will gain fame because of the controversies created by his enemies, he gain more than average wealth but can have skin diseases.If Buddha Aditya Yoga created here the person will be world famous due to some controversial writing works.

   2. Mars or Saturn comes into sixth house then person will be a hard nut to crack for his enemies, he destroys them all, he is widely travelled and have long life, but many times had hair breath escape. Sudden death due to poison or enemies is always probable. He earns

huge wealth and spends all lavishly. Taken as roll model in society and if Mars and Saturn both sits in the same house then he will get unnatural death by enemies or any other unexpected sources after major share of his age.

3. If Jupiter sits alone or with Mars then the person will be healthy and wealthy and respected in society. He will gain name from social service or Non Government Organizations after many failures in his early life. Will be of a good character and generous nature.

4. If Mercury and Mars together then person will be intellectual and famous in foregin lands and above average rich but he dies because of mental disorder, mental disease or black magic, this person must wear asthdhaty (a metal made by mixing eight other metals)

5. When Mercury joins Ketu here the person will gain fame through writing or communication throughout the world. Even if he takes birth into very humble family as low as a beggar then even they will gain nationwide fame and wealth thousand times of his family level. The few bad results are he will be husband of two wives and may suffer impotency.

6. Mercury and Saturn here gives wealth beyond measurement and two wives but potency will be the problem again here specially in early life.

7. If more than three planets forms Vipreet Rajyoga then person will be long lived and healthy will gain victory over his opponents but will gain wealth after half of his life and be in mental depression.

3. Vipreet Rajyoga in the eighth house –

The position of Mars is very typical in the eighth house in Aries lagna as Mars is also the lord of the ascendant and lord of the eighth house the house of prabal Markesh (very evil). Lagna lord can never give bad results until and unless very much afflicted. So they will get life threat either after 28 years or after 56 years.

1. Mars can only give strong Vipreet Rajyoga when it will be in the eighth house itself. The person will be long lived even after flirting with danger every now and then in his life. He becomes world famous and the point that Mare is also the natural owner of this house it enhances the energy to the optimum.

2. When Saturn and Mars both are in this house depression becomes the fate of such person, he gains great wealth from his maternal uncle and other relatives and well respected in society. He gain spiritual and secret powers in life with minimum efforts and die unnaturally and mysteriously. Very magnetic and have many physical relationships in life.

3. Mercury with Mars makes a person famous research scholar and he gain fame and money through innovation.

4. Mars with Jupiter makes the person rise quickly but only up to specific level as here Jupiter behaves like a good planet and gives satisfaction and success. He travel far and wide and mostly athlete, pilots, sea sailors have such yogas.

5. If three or more planets creates this yoga the person will gain immortal fame after long struggle in life. He will be an innovator of a new ideology or theory or something similar and if Ketu joins in here the person will attain moksha and will get divine help in his life for several occasions.

6. IF MOON SITS ALONE HERE PERSON WILL GAIN FAME IN EARLY LIFE BUT THREAT OF LIFE WILL BE THERE SO WORSHIP MOON FOR LONGIVITY.

4. Vipreet Rajyoga in the 12th house -

   1. If Jupiter sits in the twelfth house the person will be religious and of good character and will be famous in the whole world and gain both materialistic and spiritual gains in life. As Jupiter is both the natural lord and Karka of the house of luck and religion and also the lord of the same house in this ascendant and natural and lagna wise lord of the twelfth house which is also its self-sign it enhances the effects of Vipreet Rajyoga and an individual gets slow but consistent progress in life.

      He will get public support and fame and Jupiter aspect fourth house which is of mother, common mass, satisfaction so he lives satisfactory life.

      Jupiter also aspects sixth house and individual enjoys more than average health and supremacy over enemies.

      The only hurdle is if person adopts unlawful ways ,be of bad character his luck will vanished away soon.

   2. If Mercury sits in the twelfth house person will be the good combination of brain and bravery and gain money and name by defeating his enemies and competitors from impossible position he will be long lived and healthy.

   3. If Mars sits in twelfth house than there will be threat to his elder brother's life. Person will travel abroad and earned great fame and money but he gained it in later stages of his life. He will get great wealth but will be mentally tensed throughout his life.

4. If Mercury and Saturn Sits together than person will gain great respect and name in society. Not very rich but will be of a superb goodwill and anyone can give him desired money, these individuals are very simple living and faced problems related to fertility.

5. If Mercury and Mars are together in this house than person will be very brave and equally sharp witted, multi-talented and rich but sometimes gets punished by government.

6. If Mercury and Jupiter are here than person will gain his goals easily but not to the expected level so such guys should keep his ambitions high.

7. If Mercury and Saturn sits together than person will gain his name and wealth after a long struggle and hard work but the range of his success will be beyond his imaginations and will be long lived to enjoy.

8. If three or more than three planets sits in here than person will be very hard working and gain his aims very late in life but the level of success will be so big that he will not be able to sustain that his name will become immortal.

5. Vipreet Rajyoga in 2nd and 11th house –

   1. If Jupiter sits in 2nd house then person will be very lucky in money matters and will earn good.

   2. If lord of the 2nd house is in 12th house then the person will handle millions but not as his won asset, such guys will be money managers or fund managers.

   3. If Venus is in the eighth house and Sun in seventh then person will recive unearned income suddenly from lottery or any such sources.

4.If Venus and Jupiter are together in Chart then person will gain money from state.

5.If Venus and Saturn are together the person will get parental property.

6.Exchange of sign among Mercury and Saturn will make person rich through support of many individuals.

7.Exchange of sign among Venus and Mars will make person earn a lot illegally and bad ways.

8.Mercury and Venus together helps and individual to earn through court cases and business.

9. If Mercury, Venus, Mars and Saturn sits together no matter in whichever house person will be very rich.

9. If Venus and Jupiter or Saturn and Jupiter sit together or aspect each other than the person will get rich after marriage.

Taurus – This miser, the close fisted an accountant, finance, banking etc.

It is long and is a quadruped zodiac sign.

It has power in night and direction in the South.

It represents villages, cultivation, culture and businessmen.

An earthy sign, Vrishabha rises with its back.

They are conservative in money, energy and in almost everything they want the maximum output from the minimum input.

They are determined, cheerful and fond of pleasure.

They are lucky and are darlings of Goddess Lakshmi.

They are erotic but they are unwavering in their love and relationships.

They are tender of music, arts, cinema, drama, etc.

Their married life is generally happy."

Nine Planets For Taurus Lagna/ Ascendants –

1. Sun –Rules fourth house

2. Moon – Third

3. Mars – Seventh and Twelfth

4. Mercury – Second and Fifth

5. Jupiter – Eighth and Eleventh

6. Venus – First and Sixth

7. Saturn – Ninth and Tenth

8. Rahu – Depends on Saturn and Jupiter Position

9. Ketu – Co rules house seven in this lagna for person.

Planets creating Vipreet Rajyoga for Taurus Ascendants –

- Venus – Being the lord of the ascendant and naturally benefic planet it will not be able to give strong Vipreet Rajyoga until and unless it will be in extremely bad position like in enemy sign or under bad aspect. It holds Sixth house.

- Jupiter – Holds eighth and the eleventh house and being the arch rival of Venus it gives good results in Vipreet Rajyoga despite of being a good planet.

- Mars – Rules the twelfth house and creates best conditions for Vipreet Rajyoga for these ascendants.

Vipreet Rajyogas in Sixth house –

Sixth house lord is Venus which is also the lord of the first house and the Vipreet Rajyogas created by Venus for Taurus in this house are –

- Venus in the Sixth house – Person will have many enemies but he will defeat all of them but after a long struggle and many hurdles and gain money and name for his courage and mental acuity. Although success comes very late because of Venus but if Venus is aspect by other cruel or evil planets or more than one Vipreet Rajyoga forms in the birth chart than success can come early.

- If Jupiter comes into the sixth house then person will have diseases and enemies but he will overcome all, very sharp minded and skilled planner. He gains money from government and popularity also. His multi-dimensional personality makes him famous across the borders where he travels many times.

- If Mars comes into the sixth house- Person will gain hundreds and sometimes thousand times more than his efforts. He will have no enemies and gained money from foreign lands the only loophole is they are unlucky in the matter of spouse, either they will have to marry twice or their spouse will be sick or somewhat away from them.

- If Jupiter and Moon conjuncts in sixth house then an individual will gain hidden wealth or sudden wealth. Enemies and diseases will be destroyed and he will be a widely travelled person. Such individuals should marry early their fortune will take favorable turn after their marriage. He will gain more if he will take care of his whole family, he may have many kids and many siblings.

- If Moon and Mars comes together in this house then the person will have physical relations with may opposite sex gentry and he will gain grand wealth through them but love and care from the own spouse will always be in paucity. Foreign land visits will always be profitable for them and person will be of low character.

- Mars and Jupiter makes an individual attain Siddhis(spiritual powers) with much less efforts. He may not be very rich but will hold good position in society and will get protection by the government. His family will be happy.

- If three or more than three planets create Vipreet Rajyoga in the sixth house then the person will struggle with enemies and diseases till the age of 32 to 40 and after that he will gain great wealth and money in life after overcoming all hurdles.

Vipreet Rajyoga in Eighth house –

Jupiter has dual ownership of Eighth and the Eleventh house and although a divine planet but arch rivalry with Venus makes it a good candidate for Vipreet Rajyoga for Taurus Lagna.

- If Jupiter is in the eighth house – The person will be highly respected, holds high morals and worshipped by the masses for centuries. His fame will live even after him and if Rahu sits with Jupiter his name will be all across the globe and if Ketu sits with Jupiter then he will attain Moksha or Nirvana or freedom from the circle of rebirth and he will be back to source energy or God.

- If Venus and Jupiter are in the eighth house then the person born will be under the blessings of Goddess Durga. He will gain power and defeat his enemies, he will be long lived and his earnings will be from more than one source and in consistent. He can be a great politician or hold powerful position in the government. If this same combination comes in eleventh house then the person will be self-made millionaire under 30 years of age even if is born in a beggar's family or ordinary middle class family.

- If Jupiter and Moon sits in eighth house then person will earn huge wealth with little effort and without making others suffer (it is the most vital element of this combination as in Vipreet Rajyoga gain of one will be the loss of other).

  The person will be of strange behaviors, very often a day dreamer but will get great success after marriage. He gets popular also because of strange deeds. He live healthy, rich and long life.

- If Jupiter conjuncts Mars then the person will earn wealth and divine powers and knowledge easily but his fame enhances after his mortal life. During his life time he becomes a widely travelled and rich person in society.

- If Mars and Venus sits in the eighth house or eleventh house then the person will be apt in black magic and dark powers, he will have physical relations with many but his or her own spouce will be separated.

- Mars and Moons are tother in the eighth house or eleventh house then the person will defeat his enemies like a child's play and will gain good support from opposite sex and money and power through them.

- If three or more than three planets creates Vipreet Rajyoga in the eighth house the person will be a permanent character in the history of the mankind. The person will be rich , long lived, struggle at the initial stage of life and his fame will live for centuries.

Twelfth house for Taurus ascendants and Vipreet Rajyogas –

- As Mars co rules the twelfth and the seventh house so there is the close relation in between the marriage of the person and activation of Vipreet Rajyoga. The Person will get the desired results of Vipreet RAJYOGA after Marriage.

- If Mars is in the Twelfth house then person will have either a rich or earning wife. He will be very hard working man and very often do business, even if in the job he will have other sources of income also. If Ketu also joins Mars in this house then the person should get married as early as possible as his financial conditions will improve a lot after that he will gain own house and vehicles.

- If moon is in this house then the enemies will be always under the fear of such individual and if Venus also joins Moon the person will get huge wealth after marriage so they should get marry early with this combination.

- If Venus is in the twelfth house then the person will be victorious ,lover, rich and good looking. He will live a perfect life till the end but if Mars sits with it, person will be sexually driven although he will be able to keep this secret but will give away money. He can be an owner of an NGO or any welfare society and will gain name.

- When Jupiter is in the twelfth house the person will be burning the candle at the both ends. He will earn a lot and he will spend a lot,not only for recreation but also for charity ,he will never be under the paucity of money and will have numerous religious travels and deeds in his life.

- If Jupiter and Moon are together then person will gain money and fame in the early stage of his life.He will be of a good character and will have well to do financial status. He will earn fame as a spiritual teacher or in some similar fields and last stages of his life will be very satisfactory.

- Saturn in the twelfth house for Taurus ascendants is in its debilitation point and such person will be great leaders, starts from the rock bottom of their life and gain much followers and fame but money comes to them rather late in life after mid-thirties but will be consistent once they become rich. They can be great politicians or businessmen.

- If three or more than three planets creates Vipreet Rajyoga then person will be after a very long, hard and terrible struggle they gain success. They became indifference to the worldly pleasures although they gain great wealth and women after he mid-way of their lives such individuals will be the society icon.

Vipreet Rajyogas in the other houses for Taurus ascendants –

Third House –

- If Moon is in the third house the person will suffer the lack of brother support, he will gain fixed assets and will be coward. He will obliged the society and community rules but will be of fickle mind which will become sharp with the passage of time.

- If Venus is in the third house then the person will be the protector of his family and community will gain great power and wealth and even having many enemies will be long lived.

- If Jupiter is in the third house then the person will be the revitalizer of his religion and culture. He is more a karmic then a lucky person and will induce substantial changes in the society on his own will. Public took his struggles as an example and he will be much respected in the society.

- Mars in the third house is a warrior at its best, such person is a one man army he can defeat simply anyone and everyone, he will get good wealth if not much and he will be having global fame personality.

- If Moon and Venus are combined in any birth chart in this house then the person will gain wide fame and money for feminine works like, female dance, cooking etc.

- Moon and Jupiter together in the third house makes a person millionaire at early age. He will have many females, houses and expensive cars.

- Moon and Mars combines in the third house to make him inclined towards snsual pleasures, such person although he will be having beautiful wife, rich in laws , gain wealth from wife and his family, yet will be involved in extra marital relations.

- If Jupiter and Mars or Jupiter and Venus are in the third house the person will be of divine qualities and good character and will become rich and will be long lived.

- If three or more than three planets will create Vipreet Rajyoga in a birth chart then the person will be a great warrior and a fighter and will be an icon for youth for generations.

Vipreet Rajyogs in the second and the eleventh house –

Jupiter also holds the eighth house with the eleventh house; eleventh house is the house of gains so Vipreet Rajyogas in the eleventh house gives more wealth than reputation where as the Vipreet Rajyogas in the eighth house will be the game changers.

Second house as we have discussed earlier is partially evil and for Taurus ascendants the owner of the second house is Mercury, the most strange planet in astrology, alone it will be beneficial but if with evil planets it will be very evil and good for Vipreet Rajyogas.

- If Mercury comes with Mars in the second ,fifth, seventh or twelfth house then the person will be very rich after marriage (effects are highest when such combination is in 2nd ,7th and 12th house). If Ketu also joins then the person will have permanent wealth no matter how much will he spend?

- If Mercury and Venus combine in second, sixth or twelfth house the person will gain wealth through state or court.

- If third lord Moon is in eighth house and Mercury and Venus are in Sixth ,eleventh or second house the person will be a millionaire and will gain sudden wealth for his rise.

- Exchange of houses between third lord and eleventh lord makes person slowly very rich with support of friends and family.

- If mercury is in eighth house and sun in seventh house person will be suddenly rich with unearned income like lottery, share marked, hidden wealth or any other sources.

- If Mars and Moon are together in the eleventh house the person will gain more wealth then he needed.

- If Venus,Rahu,Mars and Jupiter are in the same house irrespective of the house or signs the person will be a millionaire from even unimagined and unknown sources. It is Mahalaxmi (great wealth) yoga. He is from a middle class family or from a weaker section of society money always runs behind him.

- If Rahu is in second,third,eighth,eleventh or twelfth houses the person will never see scarcity of mone after the age of 32.

- Saturn conjuncts Mercury – Parental property

Saturn conjuncts Moon – Self-made rich

Saturn conjuncts Venus – Money from enemies and maternal uncle.

Saturn conjuncts Jupiter –From religious deeds.

Saturn conjuncts Mars – From wife and in laws money comes.

Point to ponder –

The most unique fact about Taurus ascendant is this that the lord of all the evil houses are naturally benefic or divine planets apart from Mars who holds a major evil house. So Vipreet Rajyogas generally not at its full swing until they get support from evil aspect from other planets or aspect free from divine planets yet Vipreet Rajyoga made Taurus born guys very hard working and at the same time very selfish but during the course of their selfish motto they done good to the society, somewhat like invisible hand concept in economics.

For example you have opened a factory for profit motive but you are also generating employment for the other individuals.

Mithun or Gemini ascendants –

So what does a Gemini denotes?

It denotes a pair, twins, couple, partner, support and dual personality or mentality.

Being a Symbol of duality, there appears to be two diverse flairs of Gemini Ascendants ,first, the bubbly, chatty, unconventional one that dears to have fun, and the cool, knowledgeable, while the second is clever and shrewd, but comes off rather harsh at times. Irrespective of the elegance, they will examine everything and try to make wisdom of what is trendy around them. Cool and charming, they always have something on their mind. They are easily distracted because they are curious about everything, and their courtesy lengths are not known for their permanence.

The Gemini born pursues to progress the physical individuality through connotation with teams, corporate sections, siblings and cousins, family, and tête-à-tête allies.

The community behavior has an intrinsic attraction for publications, writing, mass communication, planning and scheduling, management, and all features of business management.

Gemini born is usually logical, prearranged, and chatty folk who have a strong mental interest in caring for their property and family.

Nine Planets for Gemini ascendants –

- Sun – Rules the house of courage third house

- Moon – Owner of house second

- Mars – 6th and 11th house

- Mercury –1st and 4th house

- Jupiter –7th and 10th

- Venus-5th and 12th

- Saturn-8th and 9th

- Rahu- Co lords 9th house

- Ketu- Co ownership of 6th and 8th house

  Planets create Vipreet Rajyoga for Gemini ascendants –

- Sun –Owner of the third house, the house of courage which is the natural attribute of Sun which is also a naturally cruel planet so in case of Vipreet Rajyoga it gives superficial benefits and fame.

- Mars – Rules sixth house and eleventh house which is sixth from sixth that's the reason why in Gemini lagna (ascendant) Vipreet Rajyoga in partial evil house which is the eleventh house is more powerful than the Vipreet Rajyoga in any other house as it will have the dual effect or houses and planets (as Ketu co rules sixth house.

- Saturn – The position of Saturn is very strong for this particular ascendant as it owns the worst house the eighth house and at the same time it owns the best house means the ninth house but if it creates Vipreet Rajyoga then it will make a person a divine entity after troubles and pain to the superlative level, beyond his bearings. Due to the co ownership of Rahu (9th house which is also ruled by Saturn) and its connection with Saturn. In Vipreet Rajyoga the effects of suffering and divine both are amplified to highest level so the hurdles and pain by individual are also beyond normal humans.

- Venus – Rules 5th and the 12th house and also a naturally benefic planet and in case of Vipreet Rajyoge gives mediocre results if not in very weak form.

Vipreet Rajyogas in the sixth house – Mars rules the sixth house and also sixth from the sixth means eleventh house so if in good position it will give bad results and if in evil position or in case of Vipreet Rajyoga it will give most of the wealth and fame with minimum efforts but most of the time an individual will be of self-destructive nature.

Sixth house denotes enemies and losses whereas eleventh house signifies friends and gains, you cannot simply predict easily from whom these persons will gain wealth and name but only one thing is sure they will gain now let us proceed towards the Vipreet Rajyogas in the sixth house –

- If Mars sits alone in the sixth house then person will have many enemies but he will win over them, he will be healthy although he will be wounded very often but survive. He will have immense wealth and in later stages of his life he will be very popular, popularity can come early of Mars conjuncts or aspect by Ketu. If the same combination happens to be in the eleventh house then the person will be billionaire with his self-efforts but if other Rajyogas will be missing in his birth chart then all the money will be wasted by him.

- If Sun is in the sixth house the person will be bestowed by the divine aura and will earn good name in the medical field as a chemist or doctor or any smile designation,If Sun is in eleventh house then the person will be a great mass communicator like a great politician or writer or television entity. If Mars combines Sun then the brothers will be the enemies of an individual along with many more enemies but person will live life of a king. If Mars and Sun are in the eleventh house then person will get support from the high authority people and he earn huge wealth for long run and will be famous.

➢ If Sun and Saturn are together in the sixth house then person should be very careful in choosing their doctors as they can be out of this mortal world because of the mistake by a doctor. They will defeat their enemies and gain the enemies money and popularity in society. If the combination is of Sun and Venus then the person will do well in the hospitality industry and will be the owner of more than one restaurants or hotels and wither big or small the food stuff will always prove to be he cash cows for them. (In India it is easy to find businessmen with small street shops who are earning much more than settled businessmen).If Sun and Saturn are in eleventh house than person will be long lived, lucky, rich, ill mannered, shameless and get away even after doing crimes. He show off as a non-believer but from inside true devotee to god, he travel far off land and his male kid will be the source of trouble.

➢ When Saturn is alone in the sixth house the person is very shrewd and witty and will defeat his enemies by the optimum use of mind and minimum use of strength and he will gain wealth and name from all corners of the world. The unique point in such a placement of Saturn is this that Saturn aspects his own evil house eighth with his third aspect ,twelth house which again a malefic house with his friendly aspect and third house once again a bad house with its tenth aspect which results in subsiding the troubles, diseases and enemies or that individual but due to its intrinsic qualities Saturn delivers these results with a substantial delay and sometimes slowly after the age of 35-40 the person rises in life and continues to rise.

➢ When Saturn and Mars are together then person should be very alert as even this combination will provide enhanced wealth and all sorts of sensual pleasures from, expensive wines to beautiful women, luxury cars to big bungalows but the person will be into the trouble of ending his life because of over indulgence into these things basically threat from women and wine. Despite of the fact that Saturn will increase the life span of an individual with its aspect to the eighth house at the same time Mars will make the enemies more strong and put the life under threat. If this combination happens in this house then following considerations should be examine-

- o Degree wise strength of Saturn- If Saturn is three degrees and more than Mars then the person's life will be saved but after a great suffering.

- o If Mercury is well placed and degree wise more strong than Mars then an individual will be saved.

- o Never make this individual wear blue sapphire to increase the strength of Saturn until Saturn is combusted (over 25 degrees) the only things which one can do are- Make a person wear emerald to strengthen Mercury if Mercury is well placed but degree wise weak or Vedic worship of Mars to calm him down during major or minor period of Mars. Same will happen if this combination is in eleventh house.

- ➢ If Saturn and Venus are together then person will be very rich and famous and his wealth and fame will give birth to hidden enemies, he may face problem of fertility or any other sex diseases.

- ➢ If three or more than three planets create Vipreet Rajyoga in the sixth house then the person will be famous, without enemies and rich but his life can see a sudden end. He will be honorable for coming generations.

    - • Vipreet Rajyoga in the eighth house –

Due to dual ownership of best and worst role of Saturn is extreme in both struggle and success and eighth house being the worst house of any kundali adds on to both sufferings and success.

> If Saturn sits in this house than the person will lack, support, sources and pleasure in the early stages of life. He will gain success on foreign lands and that too after great hard work. The only good thing is this that all the troubles, failures and diseases will be in an individual's life till the age of 35 to 40 years which makes a person, humble, respecting money and society and then he rises to an apex and will be worshipped by the masses.

  He will gain wealth beyond his spending capability and success beyond his imagination.

> If Mars is alone in the eighth house then the person will be brave and unconquerable by enemies, rude, firm, raise the honor level of his family and will gain from friends and foes. He gets unearned income from unorganized sources like gambling lottery or treasure. If Mars and Saturn are in this house then the person will be an innovator or researcher and will gain more fame than money and will be long lived with healthy life.

> If Sun is alone in the eighth house then the person will gain great fame but after his life, good financial position and stable social life is also there.

> Sun and Saturn together in the eighth house then the outcome will be same as Sun alone in the eighth house but the only difference will be that the person will gain huge money, name and foregin land travels during his lifetime. He will die in protecting or fighting activity I a war or warlike situation and will gain immortal fame after that.

> If Venus is in eighth house then the person's luck will be activated after the birth of a daughter, he will rise thousand times from his present position after a daughter takes birth and

he will be blessed by God for trouble free life. If Saturn joins Venus here then the person will be a great astrologer or magician, if Mars is with Venus then the person will be in the business of weapons or great warriors. The more daughters they will have the more luck will come to them if three or more than three daughters will be there then the person will gain immortal fame and wealth beyond his banks.

➤ If Moon is in the eighth house (Note moon owns second house the place of first Markesh for Gemini ascendants) there will be negative impact on the timespan of longevity so person should strengthen its lagna lord or lord of the ascendant Mercury and there will be positive impact on the quality of life.If Jupiter joins Moon the person will earn great wealth but through wrong sources and will be having a big family which is protected by the government.

➤ If three or more than three planets creates Vipreet Rajyoga in the eighth house then the person will be having the deep knowledge of black magic, dark achivements,astrology or any other paranormal science which will give him world level fame and wealth beyond the holding capacity , masses will see such person as their role model and their thoughts get followed by the coming generations and such a person will get salvation or Moksha in this life if Saturn or Ketu is alo there in the eighth house.

- 12TH house and Vipreet Rajyoga – Owned by Venus an embodiment of wealth in astrology so in any case if Venus is involved person will get great wealth although respect and fame will suffer as Venus is a good planet and also owns a trine.

Vipreet Rajyogas in the twelfth house –

➤ If Venus comes into the 12th house then the person will rise many times in the terms of finance from his family background. He will gain all sorts of materialistic comforts and enjoys permanent wealth during his life, he will have many refractive travels with family, his parents and kids will be long lived and he will gain a very talented doughter. He will have love marriage and physical relations with many women even after marriage but will be able to hide them. If Rahu comes into the same house then it will increase troubles of an individual along with his popularity and these guys are usually artists and due to the effect of Rahu the wife of individual can be of a bad character.

➤ If Venus and Sun are together the person will be a famous social worker and rich one too. He can get punished by the government and can be in prison for many times in his life but his fame will get increase because of these. If Rahu comes in then the struggle will be long but the person will become a great politician in the later stages of his life. This is also called the graham yoga (eclipse combination when Rahu is with Sun) so person can get defame also but anyhow his name will be immortal.

➤ If Venus and Mars are together than the person will be careless, brave, loose character, disdainful and sometimes fool. The lion's share of his money will get spend on enemies and women, women can easily make them fool and use them. He will defeat his enemies and get famous because of that as Mars with its fourth aspect sees third house the house of courage and with seventh aspect it views sixth house the house of enemies, therefore he holds a long struggle with his enemies but becomes an ultimate winner but very often surrender to his lust. He gain great wealth from the foreign relations and women again can cause financial problems to then such guys can keep secret women as a wife other than their social wife.

- Venus and Saturn in this house makes a person saint, they have wealth but not much materialistic desires, they are blessed by God and achieve spiritual achievements in life. They hold high moral values and stick to them, they may have paranormal powers but they never misuse them. If Saturn alone is in this house then gains will come with a delay. Money comes like anything and they spend money like nothing for charitable purpose.

- If Sun and Mars are in the twelfth house then the person will be very hard working, successful industrialist and a spiritual person at the same time. Although he see many ups and downs in life from finances to enemies but at the end he stood like a true champion. They are just like a person who wants to prove himself without any greed for example he want to be rich not because he needs money but he wants to prove that earning money is not a big deal for him.

- If Sun and Saturn or Saturn and Mars sits then the person will have salvation in his life, he wins over his senses and desires and can be called a true hermit. He hardly cares about money and fame and devote his life to his community, nation and humanity. He may recive punishment from government but will gain name cross borders of his birth place.

- If three or more than three planets creates Vipreet Rajyoga in this house then the person will have advance knowledge of secret powers like being out of body at his will, hypnotism ,telepathy and many more. His voice and personality will be influensive and even big businessmen and powerful politicians will pay him respect. They struggle a lot and may be away from the family for long time but what they gain will go with them to their next lives also.

Vipreet Rajyogas in other partial bad houses –

Vipreet Rajyoga in the third house –

➢ If Sun is in the third house then an individual will be famous sportsman or some other personality involve in the works or profession based on physical strengths. If Buddha Aditya yoga forms in this house (Sun and Mercury in the same sign) the person will be a world famous writer and will gain consistent money.

➢ If Mars is in the third house then the person will be in army, police or in the similar jobs or profession, he gain both victory and money from his enemies. He lives a successful and satisfying life. If Sun and Mars are together then person will be a well-known doctor or related to the medical field, if Mercury joins Mars here then it will make person the magician of voice and words he will be a poet or politician and will be of dual character but yet gain name and wealth in life.

➢ If Sun and Saturn combines then person will be brave and a true dare devil and will have hair breath escape very often in his life. His enemies will be terrified with his name and he proves to be lucky to escape their traps many times he will get support from his brothers and visit foreign lands very often in his life but his arrogance and rough way of taking can give rise to opponents without any solid reason.

➢ If Mars and Saturn are in the third house their will be lack of elder brothers, person will be cruel and brave and will be affected by poision in his life. He lives among the nest of vipers but yet ensure success and wealth on long run.

➢ If Mars and Venus are in this house then the person will be treated as the head of the family irrespective of his age and will take care of his siblings. Person will gain from wife and other women and will get settled in society with pride but after the age of 36-38 years.

➢ If three or more than three planets creates Vipreet Rajyoga in this house then person will be brave to the level of self-sacrifice for his religion, nation or followers, if Mars and Mercury are in these planets then person can be a bandit or smuggler but by any means he gains name good or bad depends.

Other Vipreet RajYogas for Gemini ascendants –

- If in the eighth house Moon the lord of the second house sits with weak Jupiter then the person gains wealth beyond comparison from government. Either for government contracts or projects or any sources other than government job.

- If Moon is in the eleventh house and Mars is in the second house then person will earn consistently good money after the age of 28.

- If Moon is in the eighth house and Sun in the seventh then person will get unearned income suddenly but he must donate at least one tenth of such income to charity or his money will be wasted.

- Mars,Jupiter and Saturn are in eighth, second or in eleventh house the person will be a millionaire for sure.

- Mars alone in eighth or eleventh house will be rich but Mars alone in the eighth house will be fail in money management.

- When Moon is in the eighth house and Saturn is in the second house then the person will be righ through wrong means.

- Of Moon and Venus are in the eighth house or Moon or Saturn are alone in the twelfth house then person will never see scarcity of money in his life.

- If Moon,Mars,Saturn are in eleventh, second or twelfth house then person will earn in adverse conditions for the society or his enemies.

- If second house lord and eleventh house lords are exalted in the birth chart then person will enjoy permanent wealth but for Gemini ascendants who will spend a lot for popularity the quantity of money can be low.

❖ Kark or Cancer Lagna or Ascendant – Individuals born under cancer are extremely lucky, it is the most divine ascendant in the Vedic astrology and until and unless other planets related to relatives acts as hurdles they gain everything early in their lives. As the sign ruled the opposite house or the house of marriage is Capricorn the sinner's sign cancer sign guys may have to face some conflict with their life partners early in their relationships.

Usually, these persons can be summed up as kind people. They seem quite sweet and innocent.

The Ascendant demonstrations are our usual defenses and how we manage with day-to-day issues. The dynamisms of the zodiac sign and state of the Ascendant are most overt and obvious to others. This Ascendant shows an individual's first, natural reaction to new people and situations.

They have done good deeds in their past life so no matter whichever evil house any planet holds apart from Rahu and Ketu none of them are their arch enemies as their lagna lord or ascendant lord is Moon which may suffer because of its natural attributes rather than enmity for example – Sun is best friend of Moon but Sun is a fiery planet and it can harm Moon as both of them are opposite forces, Saturn is neutral to Moon but Saturn indicates Darkness and Moon shows light so they may not go well with each other as the natural differences among them.

The past life duty fulfillment and footing up for majority of their sins give them relax life in present situation but if they are unlucky the can turn the tides by their hard working nature.

The zodiac signs are very inserting for the evil and bad houses for this particular ascendant.

Third house is Virgo, Sixth house is Sagittarius, Gemini in twelfth house which are owned by either neutral or divine planets only eighth house is under the effect of Saturn.

Planets for Cancer ascendants-

- Sun – Second House

- Moon – First House

- Mars – Fifth and The Tenth house

- Mercury –Third and Twelfth

- Jupiter – Sixth and Ninth house

- Venus – Rules Fifth and Eleventh house

- Saturn – Seventh and Eighth house

- Rahu – Co rules eighth house

- Ketu – Co owns fifth house

Planets creating Vipreet Rajyoga for cancer ascendants –

- Mercury – Owns his own naturally owned house which is third house and twelfth house so in case of Vipreet Rajyoga it makes person media king or something like that related to communication.

- Jupiter – Naturally benefic planet so in case of Vipreet Rajyoga when Jupiter creates it alone it basically gives good health and satisfaction with family love rather than super normal wealth.

- Saturn – It is the only planet which can provide supreme level of Vipreet Rajyoga for cancer ascendants as it has opposite attributes to the lagna lord Moon. It also rules the seventh house which is the place of quadrant and also second Markesh.

Vipreet Rajyogas in sixth house –

As it is discussed earlier that Jupiter gives victory and satisfaction more rather than materialistic wealth so here are the results of the Vipreet Rajyogas created by Jupiter –

> Jupiter itself in the sixth house make person struggle against the powerful and influensive people but no matter how much powerful the enemy is the person having Jupiter in this house defeat his enemy by luck and metal skills rather than pure courage. He travelled to foreign lands a lot in his life and all of his wishes got fulfilled, he becomes an embodiment of being lucky and general public remember him because of his luck rather than his deeds. He will be of bad character.

> If Saturn comes into the sixth house then person will be short of diseases and enemies and will be long lived.He devotes majority of time to social works and society and his married life suffers because of this. He suffers false blames, failures and prison also. He may be interested in collecting antique items and very persistent courage is what their hallmark is for the general public. He get sudden wealth for more than once in his life and if Jupiter and Saturn both are in this house then he

successfully multiplies that wealth many times. The combination of Jupiter and Saturn makes person spiritual,   self-controlled and yogic individual, such persons can reach the super level of spirityality in their lives.

➢ Mercury alone give skin diseases and mental intelligence. He will have enemies but will out done them with his sharp mind. Such an individual will gain wealth and fame outside his birth place. Foreign tours and settlements will bring him majority of his achievements in life. He may get interested in paranormal science and will be a dominating personality in society and if Jupiter joins Mercury then skin diseases will be cured and wealth will be magnified.

➢ Saturn and Mercury are not good for health as skin diseases or effect of poison can happen with this individual, for fertility or sensual enjoyment also this yoga is not good as such person can be saints who refrain away from sex or impotent. Such a person will be a great social worker and his fame will be long lived

➢ If three or more than three planets makes Vipreet Rajyoga in this house than the person will gain great fame, he will be a risk taker and daring personality but will be under the life threat many times, after the persistent struggle for age of 32-36 years he will gain all goods of life but if divine planets are more than the evil planets in this house he will be defeated by his enemies but any how money and fame comes to him.

- Vipreet Rajyogas in the eighth house –

Owned by Saturn the natural quality is evil, delay and grand.

> If Saturn itself is in the eighth house than individual's life will be hell like till the age of 36 years. He will be away from family, without any support and poor enough to hardly manage his both ends meet but after that they suddenly rise in life, they get Midas touch in their personality and will earn huge wealth for all their life long, they get long life and salvation in the end and will have followers in wide numbers who worship them. Their fame will be for generations.

> If mercury is in eighth house then person will be not long lived so for increasing his life span he must worship his Moon all the times and Sun and Saturn when their major and minor periods run.

These individuals have threat of sudden death but with proper Vedic remedies they can avoid that, such kind of Vipreet Rajyogas are very good for fame and money but struggles are a never ending story for such individuals, he can be a great businessman or politician or scientist or researcher any how his relations abroad always fetch him with good wealth and he enjoys all the facilities of life but yes because of one problem or another he is regularly disturbed.

 If Mercury and Saturn comes into this house than a person can be a great philosopher or artist and always advocates right changes which may be against the established systems, these individuals must get their birth chart read for the strength of their ascendant lord Moon.

> If Jupiter is in this house then the person will be long lived and religious and will do religious donations and perform religious deed many times in his life. He will not be very spiritual so will

not inclined towards the complex path of salvation. His cross sea travels will be very good and beneficial and he enjoys family life to the optimum and if Saturn joins Jupiter here then the results will become more favorable to the community and nation rather than the individual himself and he will be in process of attaining super level knowledge in occult, black magic, astrology and other such subjects but for the welfare of others.

➢ If Mercury and Jupiter are together in this house than an individual will be a writer or poet or related to similar field, he will be of a good character and long lived , he will have healthy life and sudden but painless death and he will enjoy his life completely. Normally such guys see their third generation in their life time and upto very long they remain healthy. Not very rich but ample money to fulfill their wishes sooner or later in life.

➢ If three or more than three planets create Vipreet Rajyoga in this house than the person will be extremely magnetic and very famous but their struggle will be extended to almost half of their life span, usually they struggle in the first half and enjoys in the second half of their lives. Their fame will exalt after their life.

• Vipreet Rajyoga in the twelfth house –

➢ If Mercury comes into his own house here then the person will be counted among the great intellectuals and if Buddha Aditya Yoga (Sun and Mercury together) comes into this house then the person will either be a great sports man or related to games and sports at the world level. He will be regularly sick with one disease or another specifically skin diseases but will come up with them successfully, he will have many enemies but he will defeat them all.

He will gain money from foreign lands and will get own house ,vehicles and all materialistic good in life but these guys are usually selfish and lack fame in life and if becomes famous then even negative name will be there.

- ➤ If Jupiter is in the twelfth house then person will be very religious and will have religious voyage many times in his life, he will get money and popularity easily the only loophole can be that these guys sometimes turn out to be communists or over religious and if Mercury joins Jupiter then the outcome of this Yoga will be many times more.

- ➤ If Saturn is in this house then person will face bad luck for 32-36 years of his life there will be troubles specifically from their spouse and maternal uncle and even after this age he progress very slowly but these guys are very hard working, have strong mind and heart and honest and more humanly than religious. He travels to foreign lands and slowly and steadily reaches to the top in his life and despite of having chances to enjoy life through bad moral ways he still remains honest but partial infertility can be faced by them and if Mercury joins Saturn then he will gain more by putting lower efforts and a bit quickly.

- ➤ If Saturn and Jupiter join here then the person will be a saintly king, he will gain money and popularity after the age of 36 years and will be an icon for the public, such person has followers all over the nation and their name lived after them.

- ➤ If three or more than three planets creates Vipreet Rajyoga then the person will be a paranormal expert, physiatrist , Mathematician, astrologer on likewise subject which includes calculation and research.

They face threat from the government and the society and their struggle can be extended very long even after the age of 50 years but ultimately they turn out as winner and their ideas will be universally accepted.

Vipreet Rajyogas in other houses –

- Third house – If Mercury is in this house then a person will either be a female or inculcate feminine qualities and apt in female works. The person will love animals and nature more than humans his siblings will be many and he will take care of his family. He will be generally happy and famous and will have all financial gains in life.

If they leave their birth place then they will be successful at very early age and if Sun joins here then the person will be a good politician, poet or author and will have more than one source of earning.

- ➤ If Jupiter is in this house than the person will be lucky by birth, he will get supporting environment and good opportunities to capitalize on from very early in his life. His gains are hundred times more in ratio of his efforts and if Sun joins here then the person will be a religious head, judge or great social worker. These individuals have the capability of changing the society for better.

- ➤ If Saturn is in this house then an individual gives more importance to religion, sanity and donation rather than selfish motto, money and success. He gets sudden wealth and regular income many times in his life then even he continuous on the path of simple living, he travel abroad may times and will become a great person in society but if Mercury also in here then the outcomes will be magnified along with a problem that such individuals will be sexually riven and will face impotency in life.

- ➤ If Jupiter and Saturn are in this house then the person will be the perfect embodiment of simple living and high thinking and will be a great server of humanity and needful persons. He will have an outstanding aura and will rise in life slowly and steadily, these persons are very soft hearted and honest. If planets in this house are connected with the ninth house or Moon then the person will be a saint and will leave immense wealth and women just like anything.

➢ If three or more than three planets creates Vipreet Rajyoga in this house then the person will be a great hard worker and devotee to humanity, he will serve the society and change the pre-established norms for the betterment and will be long lived, here the exception to Vipreet Rajyoga happens as if more divine or good planets are in here then the person will get his success easily and if evil planet will be here then struggle will enhance for sure.

➢ Second house owner is Sun which is naturally a cruel planet so in case OF Vipreet Rajyogas very beneficial.

➢ The lord of the eleventh house is Venus which is beneficial planet and in case of Vipreet Rajyoga gives medium results.

➢ If Sun is in the second house and Venus in the eleventh then the person either will be rich by birth or after his birth his family will become wealthy.

➢ If exchange of house in between Sun and Venus happens in second and eleventh house then the person will be a millionaire no matter how much humble his family background will be.

➢ If Sun is in eighth house and Moon aspects Sun means Moon is in second then the person will get sudden wealth, hidden wealth, unearned money.

➢ If Mercury is in the eleventh house and Venus in third or Sun in third and Mercury in second then person gains huge wealth with the support of his family and friends.

- Sun and Venus connection either by conjunction or by aspect in whichever house in this ascendant will make him rich.

- If Sun and Mercury, Sun Venus or Venus Mercury are in the second house then the person will definitely be the millionaire.

- If any three of Sun,Jupiter,Venus or Mercury are exalted or in their own signs then the person will be a billionaire.

- Jupiter and Moon in the second house or in the eleventh house makes a person millionaire.

- If Sun is in the eigth house and Saturn in second or eleventh house then person will earn great wealth but through wrong means.

- Venus in the eighth house and Sun in eleventh makes person wealthy with minimum efforts.

- Mercury and Venus in the twelfth house gives permanent wealth to individual.

Point to Ponder –

The lord of the ascendant for cancer is Moon which has two very important attributes –

1. It is the fastest moving planet

2. It has no direct tangible enemy.

Therefore, Vipreet Rajyoga struggles assure outcomes in this ascendant although with a little delay, and sudden rise and sudden fall is the counterpart of this ascendant as it is owned by the speedy Moon.

Leo Ascendant or Simha Lagna –

Firm figure with wide-ranging shoulders. You will be bright happy disposition; will have courageous eyes of grey shade, wavy hair with withdrawing hairline. You will walk upright and talk straight. All in all, you will have a right royal character.

You will have a strong, careful, forcible and watchful nature. You are laborious and possess and austere uncontrollable character. Domestic infelicity may make you distrustful of others and you may get entangled in hazardous speculations. Your pride may border on to vain gloriousness which you may curtail by exercising your will-force. You are apt to assert your independence at opportune moments, and accrue benefits.

Privileged and lucrative nature and caring human nature. Have gains and bequests and achievement through nuptial and partnership / teamwork. You will have warm understandings and a well-behaved household. You will have creative facility, plenty of conveyance

Strong, powerful nature and a personality proficient of craving command. You are forthright, unbiased and substantial in temperament. They have daring essence, motivated to deeds and hazardous feats. Gain through inheritance will come in late age.

With ascendant lord Sun they possess the qualities of King and even living in ordinary conditions you can sense the royal flavor in them.

It is a quadruped Rashi and a royal Sign.

It options to woodlands and rises with its head.

It has a huge, white body.

It exists in in the East and is solid through daytime."

Nine Planets for Leo ascendants –

- Sun – Lord of the first house or ascendant

- Moon – Rules 12th house

- Mars – Lord of fourth and ninth house

- Mercury – Rules Second and Eleventh house.

- Jupiter – Fifth and Eighth lord

- Venus – Third and Tenth lord

- Saturn – Rules sixth and seventh house

- Rahu – As per position of Saturn and Jupiter

- Ketu – Co rules fourth and Eighth houses

Planets giving Vipreet Rajyoga to Leo ascendants –

- Venus – Benefic planet by nature with soft nature so gives medium results in Vipreet Rajyogas results will be magnified if aspect or joins Saturn. It owns third house.

- Saturn –Naturally evil and arch enemy of Sun and also owns sixth house and seventh which is the house of second Markesh so in Vipreet Rajyoga gives outstanding results.

- Jupiter –Gives results with struggles as it rules the worst house the eighth house and a trine fifth house also and naturally a divine planet.

- Moon – Best friend of Sun but due to the significant difference in natural attributes becomes malefic for this lagna and rules twelfth house.

- Vipreet Rajyoga in the Third house –

- If moon is in the third house then person will gain name and money other than his birth place. Usually they have more sisters and they are very hard working and because of their hard work they becomes wealthy and famous. If Venus and moon are in this house the person will be a government officer or holding government power but their fame will decline with time and nothing like icon or something they achieve , their character is ok but all in all good for earning money.

- If Jupiter joins Saturn then person will be honest will have calculated progress, success increase with increase in life and will be a hermit and honest person living in modern society. If Moon aspect or joins this situation the person will be a complete saint in later stages of life.

- If Moon and Saturn joins here then the outcome depends upon the strength of Sun if Sun is good then person will be a saint having wealth with inclination where as if Sun is weak then person will be famous for his bad deeds but still enjoys wealth.

- If Moon and Jupiter are in this house person will be very rich and that too early in his life, he will be a great businessman or industrialist and enjoys permanent wealth all throughout his life. Regarding the effects even if he is born in a beggar's family he will be very wealthy very soon and if female has this yoga in her kundali than her father and her husband will be rich after her birth in their lives.

- If three or more than three planets creates Vipreet Rajyoga then person struggles for the renovation of society and customs. He will gain power from government and even if in the government he will be a good businessman also. His name is longer than his life.

Vipreet Rajyoga in the sixth house –

➤ If Saturn is in the sixth house – The person will be outstandingly brave and courageous and does some daring deed because of which public remember him for significant period of time period, he will be rich owner of luxuries in life and travel wide all across the globe but will have an unfaithful partner and married life will be bad.

➤ If Jupiter is in the sixth house person will be very hard working, gains from government, earn money and fame and travelled outside the nation. Get more fame in foreign lands than his own birth place.

➤ Jupiter is in its neech sign here or weak here so the person will have many enemies and diseases related to stomach ,heart and kidney and he flirts with danger many times in his life but wins over all of them. If Saturn joins fame will be immortal but struggle also increases.

➤ If moon is in the sixth house and sun will be weak and no other Vipreet Rajyoga is in the kundali the person will be under the threat of living and be very careful for the first twelve years of his life and after that will become leader of the weaker sections of the society and makes wealth and name in life. He will be very imaginative and creative. Jupiter here makes the multiplication of results.

➤ If Venus is in sixth house then person will be a lustful and loose character person, go against the society rules and behavior than even he proves to be lucky for his father and state. The person is very lucky in matter of life and finances and enjoys them on long run. Especially during the major periods of Venus he gets all pleasures from women to wine. With support of Saturn person will get magnified outcomes.

- If Venus and Jupiter or Venus and Moon joins here then person will be of good character and lucky, he will be religious and honest and with his intellectual skills earn lots of money and good name. He manages many social organizations and receives money from industry and business and lives struggle free life.

- If Saturn and Moon comes in this house the person will have outstanding control on his senses and mind and he tackle all hard situations in his life with cool mind and sharp intellect. This person is a real game changer and he turns the tables several times in his life he made his own luck. After the hard times for 32 years he becomes successful because of the excellent combination of sharp mind and hard work.

- If three or more than three planets create this Yoga then person will hold very hard times in his life but becomes successful and stand as a winner and if Moon comes into this house then he shall take care of his life and only proper Vedic remedies can save him.

Viprteet Rajyogas in Eighth house –

- Jupiter in the eighth house makes a person looser in his own birth place and winner on foreign lands. Person will gain legacy and great wealth but will be of a bad character and will have sex relations with many partners.

- Moon in this house makes the age around 60 but full life will be very enjoyable. The person will have balanced reforms in religion and sex life. If Jupiter also joins here then person will be world famous, will be able to have greater focus of mind and very determent. They are lucky enough to reach the heights beyond their capabilities in life and possess very magnetic personality.

Very well measured chances of abrupt fame and wealth are available for such individuals.

> If Venus is in eighth house person will possess dual personality he will be a good person for the society but will earn money from secret and wrong sources. He does charity for hiding his darker side from the society and will be very rich. He will be famous in common public but will not be respected in his own home. His married life will always be in trouble. If Jupiter joins he increases the results of this yoga along with making fame much brighter.

> Three or more than three planets forming Vipreet Rajyoga makes a person super magnet he will have followers in great numbers and he will gain good name in secret fields like astrology, tantra or any similar activities, he will have secret sex relationships and but they never forget their aim because of that. His work will be recognized for decades and he will be a worldly acknowledged person.

Vipreet Rajyogas in twelfth house –

> Moon makes a person highly imaginative poet or writer, very ambitious and fond of foreign travels and visits very often in life. They are good looking and opportunists and very clever.

They are more successful at foreign lands and will gain name and money although have to face several hurdles by many enemies for life long. Hard work of mind is more than the physical one and money is easily available to them.

> If Moon is in this house the person will be good looking and lazy, he will be very lucky as his father, father in law and fatherly persons like elder brothers will give him huge wealth, his all wishes will be fulfilled but he will lack fame in his life as such persons have almost nothing to say as their self-achievement.

- If Saturn is in here than the person will be very brave and often flirt with his enemies and gain their wealth but if somehow he gets mistreated by the society then he will become the rule changer and work against the established rules and customs. The presence of Moon here increases both fame and struggle for him.

- If Jupiter comes in here then it creates a Mahabhagya Yoga (Very lucky yoga). No matter if such an individual born under a very poor family or very mediocre surroundings with the increase of age his mental activeness got increased and he becomes intelligent with the passage of time and during the major or minor periods of Jupiter or moon he gains sudden wealth and income and along with the society he surprises himself also.

- If Jupiter and Venus are in this house then person will be rich beyond his expectations, he will have graceful ways for earning money and fame. Jupiter and Venus make the person super rich and great in life. He gets worshipped because of his religious deeds. Gain much fame on long run.

- Jupiter and Saturn makes a person live recluse life in the very beginning of his life; he hits the rock bottom before jumping up to the sky. He gets wealth in huge amount but yet refrain himself from sensual enjoyment; He will have global followers and will have immortal contribution in human life.

- Venus and Saturn in this house give person paranormal powers and spiritual rewards in life. Person will be highly respected and will be a great motivator and gain money from supernormal sources in life. He will be healthy and long lived and his aura will capture the attention of masses, and his control over his followers will be great one.

- If three or more than three planets create this yoga then person will be the founder of a great organization and will lead to the major change in society. They can be great researchers, philosophers or innovators and sometimes writers also but sometimes struggling period extends to 40 years.

Vipreet Rajyogas in different houses –

- If the lord of the second and the eleventh house lords are in their self-signs the person will be a millionaire after his birth his family will see rise in money matters.

- Venus in the eleventh house and Mercury in the third house make an individual rich with the support of friends and family. If Saturn is in the second house or eleventh house and Mercury in the sixth house then person will gain money from his enemies. In present days you can say through court cases or government and he also get money from in-laws and wife.

- If Mercury is in the eighth house and Sun in seventh then person will get unearned or hidden money suddenly in his life.

- If in second or eleventh house their sits Saturn and Venus Or Rahu and Mars then person will be rich.

- If Jupiter and Venus, Venus and Mercury are in the second house person will be rich.

- Two of the Mercury, Saturn or Venus gets exalted in the Kundali then the person will get permanent wealth all his life.

- If Jupiter and Moon sits in eighth or twelfth house the person starts earning very early and by the age of 30 years he will be self-made rich person.

- Mercury in eighth house and Jupiter in the second makes person rich from wrong means.

- Mercury and Venus combination in any house makes person earn money from family business.

- If Mercury and Sun are together and Saturn Rahu and Mars are in the eleventh bhava makes person self-made billionaire.

- Moon and Mercury are in the second house and and Venus,Rahu and Mars are in the third house then person will have permanent money.

Point To Ponder –

Mercury owns both second and the eleventh house so it holds equal similar value for the creation of Vipreet Rajyoga as the owner of Sixth, Eighth and 12th houses.

Virgo ascendant or Kanya lagna –

They are probable to be real-world beings, talented and deft, and can effortlessly draw upon these skills. They may be very decent with proofs, figures and particulars. They may also be quite self-effacing because of early juvenile involvements, and need to learn to identify and escalate their flairs.

Virgo Ruling native is subtle to any uneasiness or other signs their body gives them. They are enormously attentive to their health and they may relish happenings that syndicate the body and the mind, like yoga. They may be fussy feeders and be very cautious about what they put into their bodies. Fastidious may be a better explanation.

Particular about Virgo ascendant –

- This sign is a hill-resorted and is strong in daytime.

- It rises with its head and has a medium build.

- It is a primate sign and resides in the South.

- It has grains and fire in its hands.

- It belongs to the business community and is multicolored.

- It relates to storms (Prabharanjani).

- It is a Virgin and is Tamasic (a mood of demons).

- Its ruler is Mercury.

- Nine Planets for Virgo ascendant –

- Sun – Rules twelfth house

- Moon – Lord of eleventh house

- Mars – Lord of third and eighth house

- Mercury – Rules over first and tenth house

- Venus – Second and Ninth house

- Jupiter – Fourth and Seventh House

- Saturn –Fifth and Sixth house

- Rahu – Co rules sixth house

- Ketu – Co rules third and eighth house

Point to Ponder –

Since the lords of all the evil houses are naturally evil planets so this ascendants is very beneficial for Vipreet Rajyoga.

Planets creates Vipreet Rajyoga are –

- Mars – Holds third and eighth house so exceptionally evil for Virgo ascendants and in case of Vipreet Rajyoga makes a person great professional or businessman.

- Saturn – Holds Sixth house and naturally evil planet which nullifies its effect of holding a trine house also.

- Sun – Rules twelfth house and again naturally cruel planet good for Vipreet Rajyoga

Vipreeth Rajyoga in sixth house –

➢ If Saturn is in the sixth house than Person will be introvert and will face life danger and diseases many times in his life but will overcome all of them. This yoga is good for good image and respect in the society but not so good for foreign travels and benefits from them. He gains money from business and collector of the antiques.

➢ Mars makes a person out of enemies but get sick very often and had to through the surgeries for many times in his life. He arranges all the materialistic items for himself but yet hardly uses them for himself; he gains more name and money in foreign lands.

If Saturn and Mars both are here then the person will be under the life threat by poison, animals, and sharp weapons and falling from the height, he is very daring person and gain fame because of his brave nature and will get ample support from his siblings and friends.

➢ If Sun is in the sixth house then the time till 28-32 years is horrible for an individual. He may be out of penny these days, may sleep empty stomach, no support from father and friends, humiliated in society, possibility of even prison but after this life he will rise very high very quickly, wealth beyond his own expectations is what he earn and such guys have very strong soul, somehow they know that they will be great in life.

- Sun and Mars together makes an individual extremely brave and cruel here and his enemies are always under terror but there is a probability that his life will be under the danger because of his enemies also, false treatment by doctor can also cause him big troubles but he will be able to extend his presence outside his country and people will respect him out of fear more than genuine respect for him. Such person holds rude and angry personality.

- If three or more than three planets creates this Yoga then the person will be on the struggling mode till 32 years of his life, he will gain support from none, nor friends, not family and government. It is very often seen that it is hard for them even to make their both ends meet but these guys are extremely brave and hopeful and with these qualities they rise very high in their lives. They are defeated by enemies, humiliated in society and see all sorts of troubles but yet they bounce back and bounce back extremely strong. They defeat their enemies, gain supreme wealth although not many chances they get to enjoy for themselves but yet they are great persons and always remembered if not respected in their lives.

  • Vipreet Rajyogas in the eighth house –

- Mars makes person witty here, his courage will be shown in his words and writing and he defeat his enemies without raising weapons. He is blessed with intellectual mind and great and captivating writing skills and works very patiently to achieve his goals. He acts as a magnet for common public and gains much more name and fame than his ancestors and he will be considered as an icon for the coming generations to follow. Wealth is always in abundance for them and they generally hold good character.

- Sun in this house makes a person gain spiritual powers and he has the quality to know the future in advance. Although there is a doubt in the longevity of such an individual but they get spiritual attainment very early in their lives. He takes with him is past life good deeds and done some great and exceptional work in the field of society, culture, religion or nation so he will be remembered on long run. This is a very good yoga considering the fact that the karka (cause) or the basic element of soul is in the house of death and that too exalted and as soul is immortal his name will also become immortal forever and such yoga are very hard to found and even if someone has then even the full outcome is under suspicion as good planets often acts as problem but anyhow person will get long run fame if this yoga is even not at its full swing. If Mars joins Sun then person gets these attainments more quickly and in larger dimensions but threat from fire will be there for the person.

➢ If Saturn is in present in the eighth house then 32 years of such person are in misery, penny less, humiliated, failed many times, exceptional delays becomes his destiny but after this age he get complete benefits of money and family. Person will be religious and spiritual and attain materialistic wealth and money pretty easily after this age. Some secret powers from his forefathers help him. General public is inclined to see him, listen to him and follow his ideas. His troubles are very often blessing in disguise for him as he left with hardly any ego and feels the pain of being hungry or humiliated so he comes out as a good person out of his trouble times and devote his life for the welfare of the society and he becomes the legend in time.

➢ Sun and Saturn increase troubles for individual and makes his soul even more strong and after the age of thirties he gain name in some very important field related to religion or spirituality and meditation. He gets huge money and fixed assets all of a sudden but he leaves all and proceeds for his aim in life. Brave, patient and very serious approach towards their lives such guys have and they really wanted to explore the power of God and their name will be timeless.

➤ If three or more than three planets create Vipreet Rajyoga in this house then person will be world famous for some new innovation in astrology, black magic or in any other paranormal sciences and his followers are always under his spell and they not only listen to them but also follow his beliefs and instructions. He born to change the pre-establish customs so very often has top face controversies or government threat in life but anyhow these guys are great warriors and if Sun is involved then their name will be limitless.

• Vipreet Rajyoga in the twelfth house –

➤ Sun in the twelfth house make person over ambitious and he makes his life by himself as his desires and wishes are beyond his family capabilities. After the age of thirty he started gaining good opportunities and capitalizing over them, he becomes rude in nature because of the hard early life so he creates meaningless enemies but he wins over them but continuously irritated by health problems. If Buddh Aditya Yoga (Sun and Mercury in the same house) forms in here the person will hold powerful position in government or will be a great writer or editor all in all a mass communication media expert.

➤ If Mars is in this house then the fame will come after the mortal life to an individual as his deed is something very heroic and nation saving, his married life will be deserted and he gain wealth very early in his life. If Sun joins here then person will be extremely hard working, brave and tactful warrior and win over an army with little resources, His fame will magnified with time.

➤ If Saturn comes into this house makes person with a very big heart he considers whole mankind as his family and holds bad blood with none. Refrain away from fake enjoyments is his nature and donates lion's share of his income to the society and becomes very famous because of his generous nature. They can marry to a girl from degrade back ground, out of cast or religion and even divorcee women but it effects them to no harm in their social image.

Age of 32 years is acid test time for them as they get little output in comparison to their hard work. Sun if also in this house then it makes the struggle even long. HE HOLDS GREAT RESPECT IN THE SOCIETY EVEN AFTER HIS MORTAL LIFE.

- ➢ If Saturn and Mars are in this house than person will be great threat for his enemies although his death will be from an enemy only. Life threat from fire, weapon or animals is always there. The person will be a born leader. He can be both bad and good for society, it depends on other Yogas.

- ➢ Three or More than three planets makes a person innovator in intellectual field as well as technical field and a person will surely do something great in life to keep a permanent place in the history of human beings. He will travel a lot to abroad and will be famous for long centuries.

Vipreet Rajyogas in other houses –

- • Vipreet Rajyoga in third house –

- ➢ Mars in this house makes a person brave but careless at the same time. The reason is his confidence over his power he knows that he can defeat any enemy. Although get defeated by enemies sum times but always turn out to be the last man standing. He is a self-made man and gain spiritual achievements along with professional gains. He seldom gets a government jobs but get good benefits from the government.

- ➢ Saturn in this house makes person both hard working and lucky but this combination is not good for reaping benefits from foreign lands financially but yes they are famous there. Saturn with mars here makes a person a shrewd politician and his bravery is compounded with brain also and anyhow he will be rich and famous after the age of 36 years.

- ➢ Sun makes a person brave, powerful, religious and well known in society. He will be very hard working and earned all his wealth and name by himself, such guys can be athlete, policemen or some other profession which requires physical strength. Mars also with Sun in this house makes the life full of dangers but yet life will be long and he will gain authority and money because of his bravery.

- ➢ Sun and Saturn in this house makes a person risk lover and they very often indulges into dangerous sports or missions. His struggles are also with his family, friends, his body and mind and with himself. Age of 32 to 36 years he always get the results opposite to his expectations, he goes for right and do wrong. But despite of having great wealth in the later stages of life he becomes a saint like person.

- ➢ If three or more than three planets creates this yoga then person will be great athlete or world known army officer or police officer and once in his life he do something as big which makes his name forever.

Other Vipreet Rajyogas –

The owner of the second house in this ascendant is Venus which also holds Ninth house so Vipreet Rajyogas by this planet will be mediocre level and lord of the eleventh house is Moon which is also a divine planet so same results for both of them.

- ➢ If Venus is in the eleventh house and Moon in second house then person will be rich by birth and will remain rich lifelong.

- Moon in the third house and Mars in eleventh makes the person rich with help of friends and family sometimes he gets sudden money also.

- Venus in third and Mars in second makes the person suddenly rich.

- Saturn,Mars,Moon and Venus if sit together in anywhere in kundali makes a person permanent billionaire.

- Venus in the eighth house and Sun is in house of marriage or seventh house then person will gain huge wealth suddenly without any efforts.

- Saturn Venus is the twelfth house or Saturn and Moon in any house makes the person rich from their enemies, competitors and foes.

- Second house Venus, eleventh house Moon and Saturn in eighth or twelfth house makes the person rich for forever in life

- Any two of the Venus,Moon,Saturn or Mercury are exalted then the person will be rich.

- Moon and Ketu in eleventh house or Venus and Ketu in the second house makes a person billionaire, he will have many sources of income from regular to sudden windfalls.

- Jupiter and Moon in the second, eighth or eleventh house makes the person billionaire.

Tula Lagna or Libra Ascendants –

What is the most important thing in life?

Money or love?

Success or Satisfaction?

Richness or Respect?

The perfect answer will be a little of all just like in our food we need sweet, salt and other flavors similarly life is also meat to have a perfect balance in between it various flavors and that is what this zodiac sign denotes – the balance, the equilibrium, the perfect position.

Libra Ascendant generally looks good even if they will be of dark complexion their face features will be very attractive. They distinguish in behavior, dress their hair, and habiliment which suits their personality most. They like bodily ease, individual extravagances and anything that is lovely to the mind and body. They can be very convincing, favoring to use a "soft sell" when they want to stimulus others rather than a heavy hand. They are clever to pass on the responsibilities and blames to others and sometimes great meditators also.

On the bad side, Libra Ascendant can be disruptive, rude or over cautious. They may be ineffective and fanatical about enduring young no matter the cost. They may be terribly wavering in decision making. But they will be stronger than they reflect. They may turn up as soft, but behind that silky external is a will of iron. They are very diplomatic and very mindful at times.

Attributes of Libra –

"They grow tall with age and have a well proportioned body.

- Their limbs are slim but robust.

- Their advent is elegant and good-looking.

- They get bald in mature age

- They have parrot nose

- They consider the qualities and disadvantages of a subject and then fast their conclusion.

- They are positive detractors.

- They are judicious and just.

- They are also shy, sophisticated and calm.

- They love pleased and melodious life.

- They want amity at all prices.

- They rarely lose their anger.

- They like vicissitudes in their life and situation.

- They are widespread and have a soul of sacrifice in them.

- They have productive mind, accurate perception, clear understanding and pleasing nature.

- They are tender of good things and luxuries.

- Their home and married life is usually happy.

- They love their home, family and stuff.

- Libra is a Seershodaya Rashi, rising with its head rising

- They are strong in daytime.

- It is black in appearance and is predominant with Rajo-Guna (Manly qualities).

- It narrates to the west direction and options to land.

- It is critical, or naughty.

- It represents Shudra in varna.

Nine Planets for Libra ascendants –

- Sun – Rules eleventh house

- Moon – Rules Tenth house

- Mars – Owns Second and Seventh house

- Mercury – Rules Ninth and twelfth houses.

- Jupiter – Third and sixth house Lord

- Venus – Rules First and Eighth houses

- Saturn – Rules Fourth and Fifth houses

- Rahu – Co rules Fifth house

- Ketu – Co rules Second house.

Planets creating Vipreet Rajyoga for Libra ascendants are –

- Jupiter – Although the most benefic planet in Vedic Astrology but arch rival of Venus but in case of Vipreet Rajyoga makes a person equal to a king or king himself. He rules THIRD AND Sixth houses.

- Venus – Vipreet Rajyogas by Venus give more of A SPIRITUAL gains than materialistic wealth it rules first and eighth house.

- Mercury – Holds Twelfth house and gives outstanding results in Vipreet Rajyogas.

Vipreet Rjyogas in evil houses for Libra –

- Vipreet Rajyoga in Sixth house –

➢ With Jupiter in this house person will be out of enemies and diseases and will gain Government support. He will be favored by his father and government officials. He gain money from foreign travels and his relations are very far across the world. THE only loophole this combination has that such person is never satisfied for what he has and sometimes his over ambitions led him into depression. He gains much support from friend and family also.

➢ Venus in this house makes person easily rich and sometimes holding outstanding wealth but such guys lack fame and respect in life as they are disdainful because of their wealth and many times makes fair weather friends rather than true fellows. He will be long lived although sick frequently and if Jupiter joins here then the person will be very religious in the later stages of life and will donate money. THEY WILL BE HEALTHY and respected because of Jupiter.

➢ Mercury makes an individual disturbed by enemies and skin diseases and gain fame because of his opponents. His enmity will be limited to ideological differences and these guys are exceptionally good at debates. He is often mistreat in his own country and in his own community but earn good name abroad and money in huge. Presence of Jupiter multiplies the gains for an individual and he can be a big legal adviser, state or government representatives and gain power and money.

- ➤ Venus and Mercury is very strange combination here as Venus gets exalted and Mercury Neech or weak in this sign and if Venus holds degree wise strength over Mercury then it will create a Mahabhagya Yoga (very Lucky Yoga) as Vipreet Rajyoga is combined with Neech Bhanga Rajyoga (Cancellation of debilitation) so it will give heights beyond imagination to an individual he will have many followers and many enemies and whether by good or by bad he will be famous. But in the eyes of external world he will be every rich, successful and satisfied but in reality his soul always carves for real happiness.

- ➤ If three or more than three planets are in this house then the person will be good looking and brave. He will destroy his enemies and recover from sickness very quickly. Earn money and name all across the world. He will be a businessman or industrialist and will gain support from powerful people in society.

For the age of 32 – 36 years he will be nothing better than a beggar but after that he will rise with very limited opportunities very high in life. His academics will also suffer in the beginning but end will be superficial.

- • Vipreet Rajyogas in the eighth house –

  - ➤ Venus in this house will make an individual rich, artist, sensual and over spending on pleasures. He will be fond of dance, music, painting, and acting and will get expertise in one of these. Popularity among the opposite sex is easy for them but they will be of very soft heart and very feminine qualities deep inside them. But as the negative impact of Venus these guys are always under mental pressure and depression throughout their lives. The worship of Goddess will suit them and they will have spiritual attainments in life. But his spiritual attainments require support of Saturn either by aspect or in the same house.

> Mercury here makes person live mid age say in between 55-58.Such individual has strong possibilities of foreign travels many times in life is there such person gets speedy success early in life. Person will be famous abroad. If Sun is here person will be an author, artist or editor. Venus with Mercury here makes person a great researcher and speaker and he will be a great person in life.

> Jupiter in eighth house makes person long live and very healthy. Although he will be not rich but well to do in finances all his life and their main aim in life will be to gain spiritual heights and in due process person can possess secret powers and qualities for healing others. Public respect them because of their qualities and helping and generous nature.

> Jupiter and Mercury in this house makes an individual; very intelligent right from birth as a God's gift and if not then they will be brilliant in mind suddenly after certain age. They can be good writers, poets, politicians or even religious preachers. Person will be very happy in life and will go to foreign lands many times in life.

> If three or more than three planets creates Vipreet Rajyoga in this house then person will be long lived, have secret blessings of God, Lucky ,innovator, social worker, global level politician or artist and has his special place in society. If Saturn also included then the results will be magnified along with struggles and delays.

- Vipreet Rajyogas in the twelfth bhava or house –

> If Mercury is in this twelfth house then person's luck gets activated away from mother land. Such individuals are God gifted with divine communication skills and they can even convince their enemies also to favor them with their way of

talking alone. Life will be afflicted with regular diseases but nothing serious will happen. THEY WILL EARN GOOD MONEY AND MORE THAN AVERAGE FAME.

➢ Jupiter makes the person exceptionally powerful here either there will be no diseases at all or if there will be they will be cured very soon, these guys are intelligent as well as hard working and successfully arrange all the comforts for their family. If Mercury joins here the person will have celestial communication skills and will be famous for his religious knowledge. He will possess good character and noble nature.

➢ Venus in the twelfth house makes an individual extremely lucky. He comes into this world as a born billionaire and his whole life he only manages his richness. Gets whatever he likes without any hard work but yet he will be very humble in nature and religious person, he is a God fearing man who is afraid of his enemies and will have to face defeats many times from them. If Mercury is with Venus person will reach exceptional heights no matter if he has taken birth in a beggar's family even. He will be very fond of rich spouse and get easily. They are not the self-achievers so fame is not much.

➢ More than two planets if creates Vipreet Rajyoga then person will struggle for many years in life hopelessly and fruitlessly but all of a sudden he do anything so much unexpected by the society and himself even which makes his name his immortal. His analytical skills become excellent with time, innovation and research becomes his regular cup of tea and, writing or something unique to the world suddenly comes into light. They get famous at the end stages of their age and their fame lives after them. Final span of life full of enjoyments.

- Vipreet Rajyogas in other houses of Kundali –

- Vipreet Rajyoga for third house –

> Jupiter makes a person enemy free either by his bravery or his generous and skilled behavior. He will be noble person of good and divine nature and will serve the society with devotion and creates such a high place for himself that even his powerful enemies will never oppose him. His luck starts favor him after the age of 32 – 36 usually and with his creative skills and hard work he reaches a new level of their own selves. He win over general public trust and becomes a good guide.

> Venus in this house makes the person's courage creative. He shows the path of good life to whole society and pay off his family obligations also well. The person will be an artist, honest, soft and God loving person. If Jupiter also comes in here then person will have higher spiritual attainments like Kundalini activation or other experiences like wise and their name lives longer than normal.

> If Mercury is in here then the person will be born lucky, he will be a great poet or related to cultural relishing activities. He move abroad many times and gain more popularity rather than money from there, he will be rich but from other sources. If Sun joins here and creating Buddha Aditya Yoga then person will be a great author and have magnetic poster and If Jupiter also in here then the outcome will be increased many times along with wealth and fame.

> If Mercury and Venus are here then person will be poet minded, editor, author, engaged into professional related to beauty, preacher, advisor and will be world famous. He gets all comforts of life and reach heights in society. If ascendant and lord of ascendant are not afflicted by Saturn such individual will get all these results very early in his life. BUT SUCH GUYS WILL

BE SELFISH, long lived and healthy and will be successful in earning name for them but respect will not be missing.

> Three or more than three planets in this house makes an individual the game changer and if this yoga has evil planets then the person will force others to follow his ideology after gaining substantial power.

Vipreett Rajyogas in other houses-

Second house lord is Mars and eleventh house owner is Sun and they both are cruel planets. So in case of Vipreet Rajyoga they fetch tremendous benefits.

> Exchange of houses (2nd and 11th) in between Sun and Mars makes person rich by birth.

> If Sun is in the third house and Jupiter is in the eleventh house or both of these sits in one of these houses then the person will become rich from many sources.

> Mars id in the eighth house and Sun is in the seventh makes the person rich suddenly from unearned income.

> Sun,Mars,Venus and Rahu if comes together in any house the person will be a billionaire.

> Any two out of the Sun,Mars and Venus will make the person very rich.

> Sun and Mars or Sun and Jupiter or Mars and Jupiter any of such yoga forms in the eighth house the person will be very rich by wrong means.

> If Moon and Jupiter are in 3rd or 6th house then the person will be rich by earning from government but not by job.

- ➢ If Mars and Ketu in the second house or Sun and Ketu in the eleventh house then person becomes very rich but in the later stages of his life.

- ➢ Venus in the eleventh house and Sun or Mars in the eighth house makes a person rich after marriage.

- ➢ Venus or Venus and SUN OR Venus and Mars are in the second house the person will be rich but mentally depressed.

- ➢ If three or more than three planets are in the 3rd,6th,8th or 12th house the person will definitely be very rich.

Scorpio Ascendant or Vrischik Lagna –

The Scorpio ascendant or Vrischika lagna people are the influential characters and they carry a regular supremacy in their personality even though you won't find them showing off for the same. They will be imperative over the environs only with their silent occurrence besides which their characteristic and conduct will express their authority loud.

"Vrischika has a slender physique and is a centipede rashi.

Attributes of Scorpians or Vrischiks are

- • It signifies Brahmins and exists in in holes.

- • Its direction is North and it is robust in daytime.

- • It is reddish-brown and recourses are water and land.

- • It has a bushy figure and is very sharp

- • Mars is its ascendant lord.

- • The physique of the person of this lagna is well balanced.

- • Hands are generally long and strong.

- The height is above average.

- Face is comprehensive with impressive presence.

- Such guys have commonly a good character.

- Determined individual.

- He will remove the difficulties before him and proceed.

- He has a lush fancy and sharp acumen.

- He is sensitive but owns extraordinary instinctive power.

- He is self-assertion, brave, resolution, free and forceful.

- They are exceedingly sexy and have many sex partners.

- A good Scorpion person displays great curiosity in occult arts and divine experiments.

- Rude way of Talking.

- They are vindictive.

- They love to disparage Others and create their preeminence.

- The domestic life of a person with this lagna can be happy only if every member of the family is obedient to him.

Nine Planets for Scorpio Ascendants –

- Sun – Lord of the 10th house

- Moon – Rules Bhagya sthan the house of luck 9th house

- Mercury – Lords 8th and 11th house

- Mars – Owns 1st and 6th house

- Venus – 7th and 12th house

- Jupiter – Rules 2nd and 5th house

- Saturn –3rd and 4th house

- Rahu – Co rules 4th house

- Ketu – Depends upon the position of Mars and Jupiter.

Planets creating Vipreet Rajyoga –

- Mars- Being the lord of the ascendant makes Mars less effective in Vipreet Rajyoga but being naturally a cruel planet if he gets support of Saturn, Rahu, Ketu or Mercury then Mars can give complete outcome of Vipreet Rajyoga. It rules eighth house.

- Saturn – Rules 3rd and 4th house but being a naturally evil planet and arch enemy of Mars in Vipreet Rajyoga gives outstanding results.

- Mercury – Owns two signs 8th and 11th houses and with evil and cruel planets Mercury gives good benefits.

- Venus – Holds 12th house but own 7th house also and a naturally good planet so give mediocre results.

Vipreet Rajyogas in Various houses-

- Vipreet Rajyoga in Sixth house –

- Mars makes a person outstandingly brave and person will destroy his enemies and came out of almost incurable diseases because of his divine courage and live long life. He has to struggle for every comfort in his life and public image is not very respective anyhow he gains substantial money to live happy life and few times travel abroad also.

- Mercury makes an individual quarrelsome here and he give rise to many meaningless and hidden enemies in life and he may face judiciary and judge in his life. He may have skin diseases and authoritative voice, very clever and many times makes money by planning a conspiracy. He will be a good businessman and if Mars also cone here then person will be very rich.

- Venus makes a person inclined towards sensual pleasures he is many times dissatisfied with single sex partner and go for multiple ones and his married life suffers due to this. He gains parental property and money belongs to others rather than self-earning so society image lacks respect. He move abroad few times in his life and if Mars comes in then he will gain huge money and very loose character and can have sex diseases.

- Saturn makes a person mature, serious, clever, brave, and cursed for mental depression and long lived. He will be interested in occult, black magic, astrology and other secret knowledge and will have benefits from foreign relations and famous. He is more spiritual than materialistic and gives limited importance to worldly pleasures but if Mars is in here then person will have worldly desires. He will be brave and known for his bravery. He will have danger of heights, weapons, animals and will be in hazardous situations many times in his life but will survive.

- Saturn and Mercury together makes an individual impotent and under mental depression and if Mars is also weak then person hardly be able to enjoy sexual life. In other scenarios extreme inclination towards spirituality makes an individual live recluse life and all in all paucity of sensual pleasures anyhow. THSES GUYS ARE VERY OFTEN, GREAT PHILOSPHERS, researchers, scientists, spiritual gurus or teachers, yogic gurus who are devoted to their aim in life rather than enjoying worldly pleasures available. They may get popular after their mortal life and will be satisfied with their achievements in life. Venus and

Saturn also create the same yoga but difference is they make a person sensual.

- ➤ Mercury and Venus makes person good looking, healthy, out of enemies and money problems and generally famous but they are of rude behavior and dual personality the worship and show off to be religious and not trustworthy persons. Person will be an artist, author or poet and will have more than one sex partners and he will derive benefit from them.

- ➤ If more than two planets creates this yoga then the person will have many enemies, good health, mental depression, great aims, courage and of balanced heart and mind will be through any difficulty easily. Wealth and richness seems to follow him in life. He has immortal faith on God and on the basis of his courage he progress in life and gain great fame longer than his own mortal life.

Vipreet Rajyoga in the eighth house –

- ➤ Mercury in eighth house declines life span for an individual and only good condition of Mars can increase his life span in such situations person should worship Hanuman Ji and do other remedial measures for giving Mars more power and if Mars is exalted or in its mool trikona then life will be extended but any how he gets his luck activated very early in his life and he will have divine gift by birth of in the arena of artistic skills and regardless of the time span of his life he will gain immense fame and money and travel abroad many times in his life. His fame will be for centuries.

- ➤ Venus gives same results as Mercury as an extra benefit Venus ensures long life and confused life.

- ➤ Saturn in this house denotes person has done something very good in his past life as opposite to the nature of Vipreet Rajyoga he gains money and fame very early in his life from many sources and without much struggle which is again opposite to very nature of the planet sitting there which is Saturn. He will be good looking, respected in life, have family support, religious, God fearing and very humble. He will have courage to break the social boundaries for example a king makes a beggar his friend. He will be a divine personality and if Venus or Mercury joins here the person's fame will be for many generations.

- Mars in the eighth house makes the person very brave and daring and he will have to face off with life threat many times in life. Such guys are in police, can be detectives or any other such dangerous jobs and can destroy many enemies during his life. Such person has no fear of losing mortal life and will be mid aged usually and will live for the time his body will be in strength. He will be world famous very early in his life and his fame will be beyond the measurement of circle of time.

- Mars and Venus gives long and lavish life to an individual and rest of the results will be same as when Mars is alone. This yoga makes a person live life of a movie character James Bond, such individuals are very bold and lusty and will share bed with many partners and live life full of ups and downs.

- Mars and Saturn makes person struggle to an extended level in early life without any good support but such a person is like a lonely warrior who wins in the war after losing many battles and will be very respected and famous after his mid-life.

- Three or more than three planets in this house makes person holding very hard struggle for 32 to 36 years. It becomes hard for him to feed himself properly, his education can be incomplete, his enemies may defeat him, he get defamed by his friends and society but after this time period luck turns for him suddenly, his enemies will start supporting him, his failure turn into success, he will have many devotees, he will gain sudden wealth, fame and followers and will go abroad. He will be of good character even during their bad period and will be great philosophers, writers, religious preachers' authors or even astrologers. They innovate something new to the world and the area of innovation can be scientific or spiritual.

He will be multi-talented person and not jack but master of many trades, he will live very happy life and his marriage can be delayed and will get great life partner.

Vipreet Rajyogas in Twelth house –

➢ If Venus is in this house then person will be super rich irrespective of his family background or present financial status. He was a very charitable person in his previous life and he will gain everything he wishes with minimum labor. Many houses, luxurious cars, millions of liquid cash on permanent basis will be available for him. He will be famous and long lived and love marriage will be lucky for him. His in laws will be rich.

➢ Saturn makes a person deeply interested in black magic, astrology, occult, voodoo and any such other paranormal science and he will be champion in such areas and will generate money and fame because of such a scared knowledge. If Venus joins here so person will be every rich and his followers will be in large number coming from the entire world and his fame will be everlasting.

➢ Mars makes an individual a skilled and brave warrior, over ambitious and daring because of which he will have to face life threat many times till the age of 28 years and he will earn great money and name early during his life. He will have to be in prison or see government punishment but if Venus joins here then this threat will be removed. He will be a great social worker and kind hearted person and will gain long run fame in his life.

- Mercury manes a person good at debates, discussion, clever and very good conveyer of his words. He will have a pleasing personality and will have many beneficial relations in foreign lands; if Sun comes here the person will be a good writer or related to the writing field and can be a poet and good at management of money. Mercury and Venus makes a person of soft physic and very cheerful presence with miraculous voice, he will be a high profile singer or elated to music industry or cinema or arts and will earn money in large measurements and will have everlasting fame in life. If author then some of his work will be for forever.

- Saturn and Mars make the whole life struggling with the enemies. Foreign visits will be few but productive and despite of hurdles by his enemies on ever going basis he becomes rich in life and will do something very special to gain respect in the society.

- Mars and Mercury, Mercury and Saturn will give results as Mars and Venus and Saturn and Venus for such guys.

- More than two or three planets in this house makes the person struggle for 35-36 years in life and even have to struggle for survival but his struggle give him immense knowledge and after this age growth will also start slowly but speed up with the rotation of wheel of time and person will be known all over the globe. He will have magnetic personality and hypnotic way of speaking and because of which he makes millions of followers. Such guys created their history by own and will be remembered for long time in history.

Vipreet Rajyoga in the 3rd house –

- Saturn makes person proud, brave, disdainful and devoted to his religion and community, a true nationalist born with such yoga. He gains more fame on foreign lands and never care for the worldly pleasures, enjoyments and sensual life. Will be very rich and long lived.

- Mars makes a person good person in war professions. He will be an atheist, a non believer of luck and very confident over his own abilities. He will be honored by the government and well to do in matter of finances and will live good life. Saturn with Mars here magnifies the courage and wealth such person will be hard to undo and will be very famous.

- Mercury makes the person rich with the help of his brothers and friends and very good in subjects like math and other complex ones. He will be long lived and his family life will be very happy and wealthy for whole life. Saturn magnifies the results many times here but fame will be not on higher ladder.

- Venus makes the person responsible in this house and person will defeat the outer enemies but will have to see the opposition within his family but anyhow he will prove to be very successful in money matters and if Saturn joins here he will get more money and he will be apt in astrology or philosophy and can be a good academician.

- Mars and Mercury manes a person disdainful, proud, rude, and bad mood person. He will be a winner in his life and can be an athlete, army man, government official, ambassador or any such high profile jobs or profession. He will gain good name and money and will never satisfy of his attainments and will remain mentally disturbed for all his life because of his over ambition.

- Mars and Venus make a person of bad character here. He considers women as a commodity and holds use and forgets view towards them and will gain pleasures and money from women. He will go abroad many times and feed his hobbies without putting his own money. He will be rich and fame will be on good level.

- Mercury and Venus makes a person artist here and his courage takes the color of intellectual communication whether on camera or on paper. Poets, authors, cinema person, singer all are the possible profession for such guys. Person will be inclined very much for worldly pleasures and will enjoy life to the optimum level.

- Three or more of planets here makes a person a balanced and brave warrior who knows how to use brain and power wisely. Such person will be a courageous and clever protector of nation and community and he has no fear of giving away his mortal life. He will be long on struggling mode but finally a real champion will be visible in him.

2ND HOUSE ID OWN BY Jupiter which is naturally a divine planet and also rules a trine house and good friend of Mars so in case of Vipreet Rajyoga the results will come like Rajyoga only with low density of results without extended efforts.

11th house is ruled by Mercury.

- Jupiter in the second and Mercury in the eleventh house make a person rich by birth.

- If Mercury and Jupiter aspects second, eighth or eleventh house person will be rich.

- Mercury in third and Sun in eleventh makes the person rich by the support from his family.

- Jupiter in 3rd and Saturn in 2nd make the person gain parental wealth.

- Jupiter in the eighth house and Sun in seventh makes the person gain sudden wealth without efforts and from unknown or hidden or unique sources in life for once surely.

- Any 2 of the Mercury, Mars, Saturn or Jupiter is exalted in kundali makes person very rich.

- Venus in 12th house makes person rich without efforts and Venus in 6th

- House makes him rich by hard work and self labor.

- Mars and Jupiter or Mars and Mercury combination makes the person rich from his enemies.

- Mercury, Jupiter, Sun and Rahu if they sit together in any house in this kundali the person will be very rich. If Mercury and Jupiter are combined or one of these planets are in the eighth house person will be rich by unlawful means.

- If Moon and Jupiter are in 2nd ,3rd or 11th house then person will gain money after age of 28 years and will be very rich in long run.

- Jupiter   and Venus make person gain from spouse or getting rich after marriage.

- Any two of the Jupiter, Mercury and Venus are in combination and third aspects them this will increase wealth and life.

- In second house Jupiter and Ketu, in eleventh house Mercury and Ketu or Venus and Ketu makes a person billionaire ignoring his family background and financial level.

Sagittarius ascendants or Dhanu Lagna –

They will have a high, vertical and well-proportioned figure. They will have an extended look, curved temple with grey, brown or blue eyes - shiny and communicative. They will have fair skin and withdrawing hairline hairless around the temples. They will be of healthy building and will be loving athletics and other good activities.

Attributes of Sagittarius –

- The sign Dhanu upsurges with its head and is ruled by Jupiter.

- It is a Sattvic(divine) sign and is yellowish-brown in manner.

- It has métier in night and is blistering.

- A royal sign, Dhanu is primate in first half. Its additional half is animal.

- They are smooth build and adore an arch.

- It exists in in the East, recourses to land and is splendorous.

Nine Planets for Dhanu Lagna –

- Sun – Ninth house or Dharmsthana

- Moon – Ayu Bhava or Eighth house

- Mars – Fifth and Twelfth ruler

- Mercury – Rules seventh and Tenth houses.

- Jupiter – Lord of first and fourth house

- Venus – Rules 6th and 11th houses

- Saturn – Rules 2nd and 3rd houses

- Rahu – Co rules 3rd house

- Ketu – Co rules 12th house

Planets creating Vipreet Rajyogas for Dhanu Lagna –

- Saturn owns second and third house and increase wealth and struggle both for an individual.

- Venus –Although a good planet but still an arch rival of Jupiter so holds sixth and eleventh houses and malefic for this ascendants for sure.

- Moon – Naturally a beneficial planet but holds the worst bhava in kundali.

- Mars – Cruel and holds 12th house.

Vipreet Rajyogas in different house –

- Vipreet Rajyoga in Sixth house –

Owner is Venus which also rules eleventh house and very beneficial for Virpeet Rajyoga and makes the person very rich and famous and escalated his life many times from his present level.

- Venus alone here makes a person either female or full of feminine qualities and will have loose character and have love relationships with many girls in life and will get favor from them and if Ketu joins here then person will either marry or will get huge wealth from any very rich girl on the contrary if Rahu is with Venus then person will be getting same results from a girl lower than his community but wealth will be magnified. His nature can be sensual but he never do anything wrong for fulfillment of his wishes. He will derive huge benefits if worship Goddess Laxmi. Regardless of his character he will have a good public image and will enjoy everything in his life.

- If Saturn is in this house then person will be victorious but will be affected by sex diseases and poison and which can also put his life under the threat if Moon gets afflicted in their birth chart such individuals must follow remedial measure of Moon and Saturn during their major periods. Person gets rich by his own efforts and gain fame and good position in the society. Visits foreign lands with various social, religious and leisure purposes. He spends also a large and if Venus joins here then money will come from the relatives of mother and gains exceptional money.

- Moon in the sixth house makes a person long lived if no Balaristh Yoga is present in the kundali. He gains name from antiques or more such things.

  Such person is very focused on his aim and may be inclined for spiritual gains. Gain good wealth from maternal uncle and family. If Mercury and Jupiter are also well placed then person will be a great author, poet or an artist. If Venus also joins here then gains will be exceptional and will go abroad frequently in life.

- Mars in this house makes the person lucky in the matter of enemies and diseases as they both get self-destroyed without much efforts. Good job , good business lucky in fixed income but only in love affairs and kids luck eludes him. He extends his relations in abroad and gain wealth and benefits from there also. Although they spend lavishly yet they are able to save money in the second half of their lives. If Saturn joins Mars here person will be very hard working and very shrewd he will defeat his enemies in a jiffy and will be long lived although may have to go for surgery many times in life.

- Moon makes a person settle in foreign lands and have benefits from females with long life. Fame is average and he will never see paucity of money in life.

- Mars and Moon gets person wealth from maternal Uncle, he will be fond of sensual pleasures and will be of rude behavior. Strangely he loves to make enemies and get himself involved in adventures. Money comes quickly if he does business with his good friends. Generally kids are good for nothing.

- If three or more than three planets make this Yoga then person will be every brave and will remember for his outstanding deeds in his life beyond any normal man's capability. Although struggles will be there.

- Note – As Venus also owns eleventh house so the outcome of these planets in the eleventh house will also fetch same results as in the sixth house.

Vipreet Rajyogas in the eighth house –

- Moon in this house makes put the life span of person under threat (If Jupiter is weak or afflicted or in the enemy sign and Saturn aspect the eighth house then an individual should do remedial measures during the major time periods of Moon and Saturn. But within even mid-life span person gets famous in his community, country and in society. Such guys are born to complete some specific purpose in life and after its attainment they leave this world but their deeds are so grand that their fame will live after them. Vedic remedies of Moon and Saturn can extend life span up to substantial level.

- Saturn in this house makes a person lives in the nest of vipers but start getting fame very early in his life. Every single task in his life is full of hurdles but he gets over all of them easily and gain great wealth and fame in his life but if Moon sits here than one should follow the remedies of Moon and Saturn during their major period and if person will refrain himself from non-vegetarian food and alcohol the gains will increase. He is devoted to old customs and reestablishes them. He gets wealth suddenly and gain devoted followers and very frequently travels abroad in life.

- Venus in this house is makes an individual very rich either by birth or with the passage of time irrespective of the present financial condition of the person or how much poor his family background is? He always proved to be a wealth magnet and wherever he goes money seems to follow him and he gains all comforts of life on higher levels. He is calm and composes, very hard working and well established in the society. Moon in here makes a person suddenly rich with unearned income and speed up his progress. The person will be very good looking and will be out of enemies. He will have many admirers and they gain fame due to some great deeds or artistic skills.

- Mars makes a person master in black magic, paranormal sciences and divine intellect and renovates it suitable to society of his times. He gets famous at very early age and a big share of population follows him and his fame is for ages. But this is not good in term of elder brother and his own life so he must do remedial measures for Mars during his major time periods. If Moon is also comes in then the results will be magnified and makes the family of person very big and his divine abilities grows with time.

- Saturn and Jupiter in this house make an individual master in astrology or philosophy and other spiritual subjects. He seems great struggles till the life of 32-36 years and even afterwards his progress speed is very low. But his growth is always steady and by mid age he gains all available comforts in life. Either there will be no kids or kids will be of no use. He will gain honor from government and will be the head of the society.

- Venus and Mars makes a person free of diseases and enemies but mentally very disturbed, sex driven and have fear of meaningless things, they very often lack courage. They have money in abundance but they don't be able to enjoy very soon. His wealth is enjoyed more by his children. They are careless in business and family life and always in want of unearned money and they get also many times in life. They may be related to medical field and earn good name and their daughters are the prominent reason behind their windfalls.

- Mars and Saturn makes the person very aggressive and brave here and whatever he wants he will get after the age of 36 and many times his age fell short so proper remedies related to both Saturn and Mars must be done during their major dashas. But one thing is sure such guys are history creators.

- If three or more than three planets are in the eighth house then the person will be famous for generations because of some courageous achievements in his life. He will be an icon for coming masses.

Vipreet Rajyogas in the twelfth house –

- Mars in here makes an individual clever, honest, and very intelligent and such guys are experts in any particular language. Person is rich famous and very hard working but he will not have any support from brothers and he may be only son of his parents. Married life will be equal to hell but will have relationships with many females in his life which affects his public image also. Person will be a great leader and may get punished by the government but will get fame because of such activities.

- Saturn makes a person very kind he even donates his self-earned earnings for the welfare of social gains and yet he remains rich. He usually born in rich and famous family and makes his families fame more and accumulate wealth more than his fore fathers. Mars here's magnifies the effects but person will also become cruel because of his presence. The person will hold bad blood with his relatives and brothers and will be winner anyhow.

- Venus individual will be an artist, inclined to sensual pleasures and rich. He will defeat his enemies with his clever mind. Females always play great role in shaping his fortune and he will be very rich and visits foreign lands very often in life. His foreign relations fetch him rich benefits and growth level becomes high. Mars makes person very creative and very sex oriented and he has physical relations with many females.

- If Moon comes in here then it is in its afflicted or neech sign and creates strong Balristha Yoga (very inauspicious combination creates threat of life). But even after this the person will be long lived and recover from his sickness and overcome from many enemies by his own efforts and courage. He will have to hold a long rope of struggle but after a decent effort he gains money and fame in society. If Mars also comes in here then person will receive the magnified benefits of this yoga but his fame will be limited to his life time only.

- Saturn and Venus makes the activation of luck for the person after his middle age say after 32 to 36 years till this time he hardly manages to make his both ends meet but after this he becomes capable of burning the candle at both ends, he rises at least up to national level and reestablishes the forgotten social or religious belief, society gives him full respect and travel abroad many times after the age of 38.

- Moon and Saturn makes a person live a life of a saint sometimes and if other planets get weak he may face problems of insanity for sometimes in his life. But after his bad time he becomes very famous. He use to live recluse life running away from fame , money and followers but these things seems to chase hi and If Jupiter aspect here person will be a world famous hermit or saint and will be remembered for generations.

- Venus and Moon makes a person of feminine nature and qualities and he will earn great name and wealth in arts, music or any other such field. Good for money but fame will be limited until and unless other yogas for fame will be present in Navmansha or Arudha Lagna.

- Three or more than three planets makes a person possessing some hidden knowledge and because of which he either becomes a saint or lives the life of a ruler which depends on the other combinations in his chart. If one of the Mars and Saturn are in these planets then person will be world famous and rich for ages.

Vipreet Rajyogas in the third house –

- Saturn makes do work beyond mortal's courage and capability to an individual. He makes everyone obey his orders in his family and outside no matter if they had to obey him by force against their will and because of this nature he creates many enemies and his enemies are always afraid from him. His luck is not much in his favor and very often he is in paucity of security and ample money but he seldom care about such things. He very often opposes government and receives punishment also from state but all these things make him even more famous. If Venus also joins in here then person will be very constructive and use mixed ways to pursue his followers and gain respect in society. Such individual may not get substantial wealth but fame will be great.

- If Venus in this house then the person will be devoted to the safety and welfare of his family and community and very honest and trustworthy person because of which even his enemies give him respect. He becomes very rich and has many honest friends and will become world famous.

- Moon in this house makes a person skip his death many times in his life even sometimes it seems to be a miracle because Moon owns the eighth house the house of Death and here Moon is eighth from eighth so he never gives bad results in terms of life span. Person will be very intelligent and talented and will gain money and fame in life.

- Mars makes a person cruel and wanted the world to follow his ideas either by will or by force and upto some extent he gets success in that also but because of this he has many enemies. He will be rich and famous and very often he will be the single male child of his parents but if any divine or good planet sits in sixth house then enemies may defeat him few times in his life. He will have good relations cross borders.

- Venus and Moon here makes a person feminine in nature and their courage will diverted towards the constructive and artistic works if any female has this combination the she gains job, honor and money from government.

- Venus and Mars makes a person suffer from enemies for long time but wins over them finally, he is always mentally depressed and afraid from inside and unlucky in the matters related to females. He randomly gains fame and money in life on many occasions.

- Three or more planets in this house makes a person earn money and immovable gains on his own efforts and such person will be an athlete or in police, air force likewise and he love to break discipline.

Vipreet Rajyogas in other houses –

- If in second house Saturn and Mars are in with strength (at least 10 degrees) then person will get rich after the birth of son and will gain money because of his sons all his life.

- If in the eighth house there is Sun,Moon,Venus and Saturn are there the person will be a billionaire. The person will be an artist.

- If Saturn in third and Mars in eleventh or Mars in third or Saturn in eleventh or these two planets are in one of these houses then person will be very rich after the age of 32-36 years.

- Venus, SaturnMars and Rahu are in the tenth house person will be millionaire.

- If Saturn and Venus are exalted person will have permanent wealth.

- If Saturn is in the eighth house and Sun in seventh the person will earn unearned income or sudden income from unexpected source as a windfall.

- Moon in the second house and Saturn in the eighth or Moon in eleventh and Venus in eighth makes the person rich by wrong means.

- Jupiter and Moon in the eighth house makes person rich.

- Venus and Saturn in the eighth house make a person rich through court.

- Sign exchange between Venus and Saturn makes person rich from support of family and friends.

Capricorn ascendant or Makar Lagna –

So here I came to my own lagna, the ascendant of Sinners, the lagna with maximum effect of demonic powers and malefic effects from the divine planets, the lagna of those who had committed serious sins in their past lives like demolishing any religious place, killing priests or religious animal etc. It's Capricorn.

The unique observations about Capricorn are-

Liars, tendency of secret revenge, hard to judge, natural deceivers, early success almost impossible, over ambitious.

Now see the role of planets-

Jupiter-Despite of being naturally most benefic planet and deva guru Jupiter is most malefic planet for Capricorn owing two bad houses 3rd and 12th the only conditions under which it can be benefic are-

1. Jupiter sits in evil houses

2. Jupiter gets exalted in Navmansha or fall in pushkar navmasa

Sun- King of planets Sun holds bitter enmity with Saturn and it owns the house of death 8th house and it can be benefic only under the situations as for Jupiter

Moon- Malefic for Capricorn and most probably the reason why majority of Capricorns fail to have good married life as it holds vivah sthan or house of marriage and partnership 7th house

Mars- Based on placement in the chart if exalted give superb results

Mercury-Most beneficial after Venus as it holds 6th and 9th house so can give both Rajyogas and Vipreet rajyogas it is very hard for mercury to provide bad results for Capricorn

Venus- Demon guru Shukra is most beneficial as it holds a trine and a quadrant 5th and 10th house any connection in between Saturn and

Venus or mercury Venus gives immense benefits

Saturn-Lagna lord holds 1st and 2nd house so it is very important for Saturn to be strong if Saturn alone is strong in this chart it assures delayed but big success

Rahu-Based on placements

Ketu- Same

So Jupiter the best planet and most merciful planet being threat for Capricorns indicates the heinous deeds in past life.

5th house is the house of past life karmas and 10th house is for its outcome 10th house is also the house of highest activities and owned by the judge Saturn so all Capricorn lagna born always worship Venus (Shukracharya) and Lord Shiva for relax life.

Planets Giving Vipreet Rajyogas for Capricorn Ascendants –

- Sun – The King which is a naturally cruel and most powerful planet holds the worst house the house of uncertainties eighth house.

- Mercury – Rules sixth house and ninth house.

- Jupiter – Rules third and twelfth house and also becomes weak in the sign of Capricorn so most malefic.

- Mars holds eleventh house

- Saturn Second house

Vipreet Rajyogas in the Sixth house –

- Mercury in the sixth house makes the person successful with the dominant role of his enemies and his maternal relatives willingly or unwillingly. The enemies will be more a competitors rather than direct enemies and as the zodiac sign here is Gemini

Mercury will fetch great benefits here. These persons generally have great and powerful enemies and they gain money and fame by defeating them and while competing with such giants they also sharpen up their intellectual skills with their hard work. Sun here creates strong Buddha Aditya Yoga and the outcomes of the mercury increased hundreds of times and person will become world famous player, athlete, brave and writer. Fame will be of worldwide level.

- Mars makes the person rich by defeating his enemies and as an exception to Capricorn ascendants the luck of the person activated generally very early in life. They are always inclined towards earning money right from their childhood and they travels abroad hundreds of times in his life but despite of bunch of money and wide fame he is always disturbed from hi mother and maternal family. They must take care of their face during the major and minor periods of Mars and apply proper Vedic remedies to avoid any bad deeds. If Mercury is also here the person will be in army or ambassador or industrialist and will gain wealth and name up to substantial level. The person will be always afraid and depressed from inside and through his life time he will live among his enemies but always wins the battle more because of his luck than own deeds.

- Jupiter here makes a person winner over his enemies and diseases. Everybody not only his enemies but also friends honor him. He gains from his brothers and abroad relations but wealth is not much in comparison to fame, the person will be rich but not very rich. He makes and sustains good position in society.

- If Jupiter is with Venus or Mercury in this house the person will be ruthless, lazy, sensual, depends on luck rather than action and lucky also in matter of wealth. Mercury and Jupiter makes a person businessman and makes him visit to foreign lands many times in life where as Jupiter and Venus makes a person an artist and let him gain fame and money. They often don't gain respect in life as they are again the exceptions as they get whatever they want more by luck than by action but yes they live satisfied life.

- Mars and Sun makes the person very brave and winner but he has threat from weapons and fire throughout his life. His bravery becomes his hallmark for the society. He is not very lucky but he gains name and money and change his luck by his actions and hard work. Mars and Jupiter or Sun and Jupiter magnify these outcomes.

- Three or more than three planets in this house makes a person go against the tides, he changes the per running customs and laws in the society and people are bound to follow him either by respect of by fear. His childhood is afflicted by various fears and he struggle all his life to make others suffer the same. He may earn much money but not respect in good terms.

Vipreet Rajyoga in the eighth house –

- Sun in the eighth house doesn't makes a person long lived and this is also an exception as eighth lord in the eighth house in any kundali always give very long life but here Sun gives more than average life say 55-60 years but also threat from fire. Such person will be very brave, courageous warrior, and still very humble and down to earth. He gets the spiritual attainments with minimum efforts. He gets sudden unearned income many times in life but he spends all. He makes the mass go back to the forgotten customs and very often travels abroad in his life. His fame lives even after him and if somehow Jupiter joins here the outcomes will be enhanced.

- Jupiter makes a person much respected, famous even across sea, and his luck activated on foreign lands. Although he is not very rich but ever see paucity of money in his life. He will be spiritual and will live long if Mercury also in here but dies unnaturally because of lungs or air ailments.

- Mercury alone gives person long life but a sudden and painless end to his mortal life. His luck will activate early but away from birth place and he will be rich in life. If Sun comes in here then person will be a world famous author and his work will be remembered for ages but then his struggles may get enhanced.

- Sun and Mars makes a person rich through the business of weapons, medial equipment or medicines or metals. He will be very hard working, patient and honest. But he will have great threat from fire to his work place, house and to even his life. He will be very famous and served by many powerful people in the society; he will have an effective personality and magnetic character and somehow never care for money or fame instead of having them in substantial magnitude.

- Mars and Jupiter makes the person extremely spiritual he moves ahead of fire and death he gets all the outcomes as mentioned for Sun and Mars.

- Jupiter and Saturn make a person extremely magnetic and he gains thousands and lakhs of followers with minimum efforts. He will have a divine blessings and enjoying all comforts of life without indulging into them.

- Three or more than three planets create Vipreet Rajyoga then person will be unconquerable, outstanding in arts and very imaginative. He led to some new innovation, research or something related to science but if Sun involves in these planets then life span will be affected so in the major and minor time periods of Sun proper Vedic remedies should be done. But irrespective of his time of life his fame of life will be for generations.

- Twelfth house gives same results as the third house as owned by Jupiter but the only difference will be more struggles with more success for man.

Vipreet Rajyogas for twelfth house –

- Sun makes the person a hidden hunter in this house rather than a courage full warrior who changes major and old beliefs of society. Jupiter with Sun increases the results whereas Mercury with sun increases the fame and popularity for ages.

- Mercury makes a person live healthy and enemy free life but his luck gets activated away from his birth place.

- Mars or Saturn of both is in this house an individual will be an uncrowned King. He gains so much respect and fame of his followers that they are ready to give anything on his order. His childhood and youth are very struggling but after his mid age he lives good life.

- If three or more than three planets are in this house then an individual struggle for 32-36 years of his life and after that takes steady rise and becomes world famous. If Venus also comes in here then person will be a businessman, Jupiter and Ketu makes him the head of any religious institution or community. Sun and Mercury makes him great warrior.

Vipreet Rajyogas in the third house –

- Jupiter delay the success in this house and general masses consider an individual as a lazy person but such guys are hidden genius and they gain success after the age of 28 in life generally.

- Mercury makes the person having success very early and even in teenage also. They get popular up to the national level at least and gain ample money to fulfill all their wishes. Their enemies are also very powerful and wealthy people but they win over their enemies easily. If Jupiter or Venus also comes in here then visiting to foreign lands many time in their lives becomes their destiny and. With the passage of time they became great social workers and annexed to welfare firms. He will get married at early age and he will have feminine qualities and wife will be good for him.

- Sun makes a person long lived and brave. He will be good in writing, sports or in other brave deeds and will get fame because of such things in life. These guys possess hidden power of predicting future. He very often gets unearned and sudden wealth. If Sun accompanies Jupiter then person will be happy in married life and his fame will life after his mortal life. Such persons get success at the early age.

- Mars makes a person rich with the help of brothers and friends but although ample money will be at his disposal yet person is unable to enjoy all comforts of life. Person will have good relations abroad and bad his birthplace he will be rich and famous.

- Sun and Mercury makes a person brave and excellent manager especially in war or in army. He gains success and fame pretty easily and such guys can be editor, critics or somehow related to mass media. They are considered as selfish. They started earning money at early age but their fame increases only after decent time.

- Mars and Sun either in the third or in the second house makes a person very daring, brave, rude, hardworking and playing with destiny. He gains fame very easily but within the limited arena or among specific gentry of people. He will have no elder brother or will gain nothing from elder brother. Very healthy life but sometimes may go through some surgeries. They die unnatural death and will have good life span. May have to struggle foe legacy and property but money flow will be constant in life.

- If three or more than three planets sits in this house then person will be soft, brave, cultural , lawful and will apt in one of these qualities on the higher ladder of the society. Person will have to struggle for long but finally he will have everything he wishes.

Vipreet Rajyogas in the other houses –

Second house is owned by Saturn and Eleventh house by Mars.

- If second house has three or more than three planets in this house the person will be rich beyond his imagination but this money can't give him satisfaction. He will be honored by government, have every comfort of life, houses everything but yet he always remains sad throughout his life. The person will be risk loving and selfish and that's why people often talk bad about him behind his back. Such person rises in life after 32-36 years and his works supposed as good ones in history.

- Three or more than three planets in the eleventh house make the person a self-made man. The parents and family are always stressed because of his very high and almost unconquerable expectations. He does all sorts of good and bad things for his success. Such guys are super selfish and for earning a penny they can make others suffer dollars. He is clever, efficient and a real table turner of his own kind. His struggles started right from his childhood as generally such person take birth in humble or ordinary family. He travels abroad for hundreds of times and becomes very rich but because of his over expectations he always lacks self-satisfaction.

- Mars in second house and Saturn in eleventh house or any relationship in between Mars and Saturn either by combination or by aspect in the second or eleventh house make the person very rich from early age.

- Saturn,Venus and Mars in second, third or eleventh house person will be very lucky in money matters. He will earn great wealth by his own efforts.

- Two of the Saturn, Mars or Mercury if in their exaltation signs the person will be a billionaire.

- Saturn in the eighth house and Sun in the seventh makes the person suddenly rich.

- If Sun in second and Saturn in the eighth or Sun in the eleventh and Mars in the eighth house the person will be a millionaire but through wrong ways.

- Saturn and Moon combination makes a person gain from mother, mother land, servants or maternal relatives.

- Jupiter and Mars annexed through yoga or aspect makes person rich from friends, brothers and other relatives.

- Mars is connected with tenth house or Venus the person will gain from government.

Aquarius ascendant or Kumbha Lagna –

The Rashi Kumbha or sign Aquarius signifies a man holding a pot. Its face is dark-brown. It is average build and human zodiac sign which is strong in day time. It recourses to deep water and is an airy sign.

It rises with its head and is Tamasic (evil). It dominates Shudra, the fourth Varna and direction is west and ascendant lord is Saturn.

Aquarius or Kumbha is the punya or divine sign owned by Saturn. These guys comes into this world after squaring off their sins in the past lives when they had taken birth into the Capricorn or Makar ascendants and now it's time for them to gain rewards of their efforts.

This sign is co ruled by Rahu so the position of Rahu is very important and sometimes more important than the lord of the ascendant even.

Attributes of Aquarius are –

- People born with this lagna or ascendant are ordinarily tall with full build.

- They are stout.

- Their appearance is fair and presence is handsome.

- They are brainy.

- They are decent atmosphere readers.

- They are good decision makers.

- They are sluggish in accepting and analyzing things, but once they get at them, they can grip them with ease and sureness.

- They have a wide-ranging viewpoint and human concern.

- They are generous, human and careful.

- They are circle conscious.

- They are earmarked in nature and great censors.

- They have good intuitional ability.

- The married life of a Kumbha native is pleased only if one's spouse is as brainy as oneself.

- These folks are unwavering in their liking but they do not show it.

Nine Planets for Aquarius ascendants –

- Sun – 7th house

- Moon – 6TH house

- Mars – Owns 3rd and 10th house

- Mercury – Rules 5th and 8th House.

- Jupiter – 2nd and 11th houses.

- Venus – Lord of fourth and 9th house

- Saturn – Lord of 1st and 12th house.

- Rahu – Co rules house one

- Ketu – Temporary Lord of 8th and 10th house (only during his own time period.

Planets giving Vipreet Rajyoga for Aquarius or Kumbha Lagna or ascendants.

- Mars – Owns third house and the tenth house but as first house are evil and Mars is naturally a cruel planet it gives good result in Vipreet Rajyoga.

- Mercury – Owns Eighth and Fifth house as It is a neutral planet and first sign it holds is divine it can give good results in Vipreet Rajyoga only when it will be sitting with any cruel or evil planet.

- Moon – As it is the owner of the sixth house.

- Saturn – Also lord of the ascendant but at the same time naturally evil planet also rules the twelfth house so gives good results in Vipreet Rajyoga but after a long struggle.

Vipreet Rajyoga in Sixth house –

- Moon is not very good in this house as the only benefit is gain from maternal side. The effect of diseases and enemies will be there. If more Rajyogas or Vipreet Rajyogas are there then this position will be beneficial.

- Mercury in this house makes the person extremely intelligent. Religion. Law, astrology or some related fields becomes his expertise. He makes rules for others but never follow by himself. He is very good at speaking skills and can make reality a confusion and confusion a real and wealth comes with his skills only. Education will not be much but he will gain all his comforts easily. He will be a great poet or writer if moon joins in here.

- Saturn in this house makes a person healthy and having hair breath escape many times in his life. He will be honored all across the globe, wealthy, courageous, visitors to foreign lands and a self-made man. His sound of voice is magmatic and he is interested in changes. If lord of the ascendants is weak then do proper remedial measures as per the Vedas to gain long life. Moon here with Saturn makes the outcomes even more but very bad health in childhood, metal depression in life so demands remedies.

- Mars is weak or neech in this house and so as bad results gives many enemies but ultimately he comes out as a winner. The exalted aspects of Mars on twelfth house make the person famous on foreign lands. He will become very rich by his own efforts and courage.

- Mars and Moon in this house makes a person get benefits from females in life. The person will be a high profile artist or professional. He gain much higher in the comparison of his efforts and very often visits abroad in life.

- Mars and Mercury make the person destroy his enemies by the use of his brains rather than strength. He will a philosopher, mathematician, engineer or any other relevant professional and gains both money and name because of this. Although the person will have problems related to skin diseases but yet he will be long lived.

- Saturn and Mercury make the person high thinking but simple living kind of a person. He is a saint who devotes his life to the rejected and sick section of the society and will gain great name because of that. He is very self-satisfying person and yet will never see paucity of money in his life.

- If three or more planets are in this house then person will have struggle from 32-36 years of his age, his education may take a break, he may change many jobs and places but after this age he gets all the pleasures of life and will be very famous although may receive punishment from government.

Vipreet Rajyogas in the Eighth house –

- Mercury in the eighth house makes an individual a world level speaker, artist, musician, actor, singer or musician. His fame goes beyond his mortal life. He places himself on the top of the ladder and gain the fame world wide. If Moon also joins in here the person will get magnified benefits and he will be a billionaire but all these things comes to happen after the age of 32-36 years and pace up with the passage of time.

- Saturn in the eighth house give the person very long life and such persons possibly see the son of their grandson also. His fame will be not at an international level nor he will be very rich but he will be widely respected in the society and will have ample money to gain all comforts for his very big family and he will have a long and happy family life. His fame and money increases with his life and if mercury also joins here than person will be a good preacher, apt in hidden sciences, good at black magic or astrology or any such art and will be under mental pressure all the times. He may face the problem of fertility or potency in life.

- Mars in this house makes a person, fastidious, brave, daring and he hardly consider anything important more than his own wishes and because of these qualities he becomes world famous. He very often puts himself in the spot of bother but he successfully tackles the hurdles in his way. Mercury also here adds the brain to his bravery and makes him little more diplomatic which helps him in increasing his popularity and wealth.

- Moon makes the person win over his senses to the supreme level of spirituality like Kundalini (hidden powers in human) and Samadhi (Art of living without water, food and air). He will be healthy and good looking but his life span will be under doubts if lord of the ascendant is weak so proper Vedic remedies must be done for that. If Mercury or Venus is also there then the person will be a great actor and he will have wealth beyond measurements.

- Mars and Moon makes a person an ever winner in life, he can be in army or police and will remembered for his good deeds. He will have great wealth and he may have relationships and benefits from many women. But life span will again be under scrutiny so proper Vedic remedies will be required. He will be self-made man and will be remembered for ages to come.

- Moon and Saturn makes the person very serious, clever and spiritual but always under mental depression. Although life will be full of struggles but he will have all comforts of life from direct sources. Person will be long lived and if Mars also joins here the person will be on the very high level of divine attainment and will get great respect in society.

- Three or more than three planets in this house makes an individual cross every barrier of fame and person will be world famous as an athlete or actor or spirituality and his fame will be immortal with permanent wealth for his life.

Vipreet Rajyogas in the twelfth house –

Saturn in this house is also the lord of the ascendant and so it gives person useless tensions related to family and friends to the person. He will be thin and will have diseases and enemies also but yet he will be very lucky as all his wishes fulfilled sooner or later with his own efforts. He will be of good character and very famous and all his aims completed in his life. He rises slowly but steadily and reaches the top of the hill finally.

- Mars is exalted here so his expenses are turned into his incomes or his expenses prove to be his investments and from there he derived many gains in life. But the bad effect will be that person will be over hard working and somehow willingly or unwillingly hurting his own self. More Vipreet Rajyogas or Rajyogas makes a person to have access to thi higher spiritual attainments and great growth of the soul. His good deeds in past lives make him gain spiritual powers at very early age in this life. Saturn or Moon must be related to 6th.8th,9th or 12th house then he will gain success in spirituality beyond imagination.

- Moon makes even enemies of the person his friends because of his generous and kind nature. Their self believe is so high because of which they can attain any of their wishes in life. They get the high post and wealth easily and if Saturn is in here then the results get magnified but obviously with little delay and increased efforts. The person will be widely travelled and very famous.

- Mercury makes a person being famous because of his love not only for a particular partner but his whole personality will be very pleasing and loving. Living life as anything like astrologer, preacher, leader or lawyer no matter whatever he does he will do with a particular refined method? These guys are very confused in their early life and the level of confusion will be so high that people will start considering them fools but later on the same people will worship them as teachers. Saturn makes the person over passionate towards the hidden knowledge and paucity of sex and worldly pleasures.

- Mars and Moon makes a person lucky in female matters and they often involved with females from rich and good backgrounds and gains from them. He can be anti-government or even anti-social sometimes and get punished for his actions but anyhow he will be rich and very much of a communist mentality and will put religion over and above everything. Person will have many enemies but after a long struggle he will be able to destroy them all. He progress in lie with the help of his elder brothers and if Mercury also comes in here the person will be very rich the only loophole is that more than one marriage is possible.

- Mercury and Moon in this house makes a person very clever, attractive, and good in vocal skills, poet or artist and makes them earn huge money. The person will be out of enemies and lives healthy. Foreign visits also happen many times in life.

- If three or more planets sits in this house then person will struggle for 32 to 36 years in life and that struggle is so long and hard that even an individual starts to believe that he is unlucky but after that he takes a great rise as all the failures developed the perfection in him and he makes the use of the opportunities at his disposal to the utmost. Despite of the fact that his life will have continuous ups and downs but his wealth and comforts will always be there. He will have no enemies generally and average health for life.

Vipreet Rajyoga in the third house –

- Mars gives very strong and sturdy personality to a person mixed with courage. His enemies are afraid from him and he seldom fined any direct enemy. Mars aspects sixth house from here which makes him free from opponents and diseases. The person will be world famous and if Moon also joins in here the person will get benefits from maternal uncle and if Moon is alone in this house then person's progress will be with the help of his sisters and aunts. He will be rich and gain name.

- Mercury makes a person a magician of words, such guys can explain and preach even the toughest subjects also with ease. If Mars also joins here the person will be an engineer or mathematician and will earn substantial money and fame.

- Moon and Mercury makes a person famous in the arena of writing. He can be a descriptive or mystery or fiction writer. This person is very spiritual and able to keep his readers and society under his spell. He will have irritating personality and success comes to him at an early age. Moon and Saturn results will be same as Saturn alone but only mental depression and fame will be increased.

- Mercury and Saturn make a person, liar, non-trustworthy, pilferer, and lazy but of very sharp mind. They lack self-respect and dignity but they will have great wealth and somewhat negative fame or earn bad name.

- Three or more than three planets here make an individual world famous no matter how they reach at that point either by honesty and hard work or by lies and luck but they will be there for sure.

Other Vipreet Rajyogas -

Both second and eleventh houses are owned by Jupiter.

- Jupiter in the second or in the eleventh house makes the person very rich right from his birth and after his birth his family's financial conditions improves.

- If Moon and Mars sits in second or eleventh house the person will be a millionaire after marriage.

- If Saturn and Mars in the first house and Jupiter is in the eleventh the person will be super lucky in terms of money.

- If Jupiter is in one of Sagittarius or Pisces and Saturn is in Aquarius or Capricorn person will get sudden wealth and a huge one after the age of 32.

- Jupiter in the eighth house and Sun in the seventh house then the person will surely receive sudden and unearned income.

- Jupiter in the eighth and Mercury in the second makes the person very rich but through wrong ways.

- Mars in the eleventh house and Jupiter in the third the person will be rich because of the support from his elder brothers.

- If in any of the trine or quadrant houses sits Sun, Rahu,Saturn,Mars and Mercury person will be wealthy for sure.

- Jupiter and Mars combination in second, third, eleventh, twelfth or sixth house makes an individual rich.

- Jupiter in the eighth house and Mercury in the eleventh house make the person rich through ground and soil.

- Moon and Jupiter in 2nd,6th and 12th house makes the person earn through his enemies and many ways.

- Jupiter and Mars combination gives parental wealth to person.

Pieces ascendants or Meena Lagna –

PISCES is the final sign of the zodiac and rendering to Brihat Parashara Hora Sastra, Pisces "denotes resolution." The native with this lagna or Ascendant is in a conclusive stage this lifetime; this is not a accomplishment point in reverence to their soul's voyage, but in admiration to who they are, and what their lives involve of.

Capricorn comes into this world to foot up for their sin, Aquarius to receive gains after squaring off their sins and Pisces for ultimate goal of their soul circle of being human.

What Meena Lagna denotes –

- The veils-scales among Two Worlds, the spiritual and material.

- Bridges route to the world of the ancestors.

- Bridge amid of the mortal world and the spiritual world.

- Fancy and visions which are fundamental parts of the astral-material bond.

- Spiritual Guidance toward the development of personal, interior Wisdom and Compassion (Guru).

- The connection between the waking life and human world.

A per Maharishi Parashara –

- Mostly short in height but they are plump with short hands and feet.

- By nature ethical, fidgety, full of fancy and fond of loving life.

- They are truthful, caring and obliging.

- Sometimes being over-liberal and over-generous.

- They often hinder their own growth.

- They are happy in spending money to help others and for generous causes.

- These guys are not stable.

- They may have many jobs and professions.

- The married life of a Pisces native is usually happy

- They have jealous nature.

Attributes of Pisces ascendant –

Meena resembles a pair of fish, one tailed with the head of the other in other words it is the science of completion in between the spiritual and the mortal world.

- This sign is powerful at night.

- It is a water sign and is major with Sattva-Guna (divine qualities).

- It signifies firmness and is a water-resorted.

- It is footless and has a average build.

- The direction is North and rises with both head and back.

- It is ruled by Guru or Jupiter.

Nine Planets for Pisces or Meena Lagna –

- Sun – Rules 6th house

- Moon – Owns 5th house

- Mercury – Rules 4th and 7th houses

- Mars – 2nd and 9th house

- Jupiter – 1st and 10th houses ruled by him.

- Venus- 3rd and 8th house

- Saturn – 11th and 12th houses

- Rahu – Co rules 12th house

- Ketu – Subordinate ruler of 9th house.

Planets giving Vipreet Rajyoga for Pisces Lagna –

- Venus – The worst planet for this ascendant and despite of being a naturally beneficial planet it is very good when in Vipreet Rajyoga for this Lagna as Jupiter holds arch rivalry with Venus the parallel teacher of Demons. Owner of 3rd and 8th houses.

- Sun – Very good in Vipreet Rajyoga as being a naturally cruel planet. Rules 6th house.

- Saturn – Naturally evil planet and owe 12th house.

Vipreet Rajyogas in the sixth house –

- Sun makes a person victorious over is enemies even from nowhere situations. He will be punished by his father and the government or no support from them at all. He will have diseases but he will have a careless attitude towards them which sometimes makes their body thin and weak. He gains not much from his external relationships but many times goes abroad in life. He will gain fame and money by his own hard efforts. These persons are respected even by their enemies and will be lucky in money matters.

- Venus in the sixth house makes the person super lucky in the matter of money and other worldly comforts. His every worldly desire fulfilled. He can be sick because of over indulgence in recreation. He will be an individual of no dignity and will do charitable deeds just for show off and without any natural sympathy or feeling. He will be a great businessman and will get fame because of his earnings and profession. He will be abroad many times and his success will be based on the manners he ditches his partners and others who believes on his words. He will be backstabber for his profits. If Sun is in here, his show off nature and dishonesty will be subsided slowly and he will be able to gain respect.

- Saturn in the sixth house gives longevity and makes him high profile singer, writer, astrologer, expert in mysterious arts or poet. The person will be very devoted to his profession as saints devoted to their worships. This is highly auspicious position and it gives person wealth, fame and spiritual attainment but yes after a very hard work but person will live happily fulfilling all his dreams.

- Venus and Saturn in this house will bring all sorts of gains to an individual. The person will be long lived and will have healthy life. His enemies will destroy themselves without much of his efforts. He will have divine blessings on him and he will live a perfectly balanced life in between spirituality and mortality for long time. He will be very charitable and will be remembered for his deed for the long time in future.

- If three or more planets are in this house then person will gain wealth on great scale and immortal fame but after 32 years of age which can extend to 36 years also.

Vipreet Rajyogas in the eighth house –

- Venus here makes a person very intelligent, long lived, possess brain powers and will be a blessed man. He will never be out of money and richness and he will be the owner of many houses and will be head of many firms. After the age of 28 years he starts progressing in life and as his age goes on he climbs the stairs of success continuously. He will be a great social worker and will gain support from his family and friends.

- Sun may not make person long lived but his life will be very healthy although proper remedies of Lagna lord if Lord of the ascendant is not strong must be done during the major and minor periods of other Markesh (Lord of the second and 7th house) to enhance life as Sun never be the cause of end for these persons. He will have great threat from fire and enemies and he may get great defeat from them. The fame will be great and person will gain money from his enemies and opponents. Venus also makes the person long lived and the outcomes will get enhanced.

- Saturn in this house makes a person long lived, holding divine powers and a blessed soul. His each and every aim is full of numerous hurdles and while removing his hurdles he develops many qualities in himself and at the end he will be winner. If Venus is also here then the person will have great gains in his life and money and fame will be like nothing for him.

- Sun and Saturn makes a person long lived, struggling, self-satisfied and very good. Such guys can even win God's blessings by their own efforts. He will be rich at an early age and will get fame also. He will be out of enemies and diseases and irrespective of his present family background he will rise hundred times in his life. From 32-36 years he struggles for his survival and when at his rock bottom he suddenly springs up and gains the achievements beyond his imaginations.

- Three or more than three planets creates this yoga person will be an expert in black powers,astrology,paranormal art or something like this only and will be very brave and will have divine qualities. Such persons will win over all their hurdles and will become great in life. His fame will run for ages.

Twelfth house Vipreet Rajyogas –

- Saturn makes the person makes money from abroad rather than his mother land. He will have many enemies and person will be drained out in defeating them. He will be healthy generally. He will be respected by his enemies because of his committed and hardworking attitude and will be rich and gain all comforts of life on his own. He will be famous for the longer period of ages.

- Venus makes the person super rich here, whether he will try for it or don't try, he work or don't work. Generally he takes birth in a rich family and even if he takes birth in a family of humble financial condition or even a beggar then even he will be a billionaire for sure by his youth and money will come from all the known and unknown sources, if a girl has this yoga in her kundali marry her and her husband will be rich for sure. If Saturn will also be here then person will be very well behaved even after being super rich but all these things will come to him after 32-36 years of life but Saturn will also increase fame here. He will go abroad many times in life.

- Sun makes a person famous at least to the district level. He will be very brave and victorious but will have threat of fire. He will be punished by government and will be a real dare devil and will take the bull by the horns. He will have long struggles, wealth and respect and if Saturn also comes in here the outcomes will be increased.

- Sun and Venus makes an individual an industrialist, leader, politician or high profile government official. He will have no diseases and enemies and will gain money and fame. He will be lazy and well settled in his life.

- Three or more than three planets in this house makes the person struggle on long run till32-36 years of his life when he gets almost no outcome at all in relation to his hard efforts. He will get support from none, neither from his family nor from his friends but after this age he will be on the acclivity of success on long run. Patience and courage becomes the counterpart of their nature and with these tools they will on an apex in the later stages of his life. He starts getting output more than his efforts, his enemies face sudden defeat from him and he gets sudden money also. He becomes clever, experienced and brave because of the failures of life and his prediction power also magnifies and his fame lives after his mortal life.

Vipreet Rajyoga in the third house –

- Venus makes a person brave, hardworking and intelligent. He will be in mass media, lawyer or preacher; he can also be poet not writer. Such guys are over ambitious and that is the reason why the fell short of their expectations although will gain ample money and fame in life. They are long lived and caring for family.

- Sun in the third house makes the person dual faced. One faces which is exposed to the world where people think that they are coward, lazy and weak and another face which is unknown to the world where they are brave and clever and many times he see failures in his early life. They will have many enemies and will make them struggle on an extended frame but they will win in the end. If Mercury is in this house then the person will be a writer or editor or related to this field only and if Venus is with Sun then person will be a good business man of precious metals, medicines or cosmetics and beauty products. He will travel abroad and will gain money and fame in the second stage of his life.

- Saturn in this house makes the person earn with the help of brothers, relatives and friends. The person will be brave and constructive in nature and will gain fame because of social works. He will be respected in his homeland and abroad and will earn great money in life. His fame will be limited to his lifetime only.

- Sun and Saturn makes the person struggle from the world and also from himself here degree wise strength will play the major role in crafting the personality of an individual. His effort goes to waste several times in life. He will have to struggle with his enemies for his life time but his bravery gives him real fame in life.32-36 years of life will be struggling and after that his time turns and he becomes money owner and travel abroad.

- Three or more planets here make a person struggle a lot from his enemies and from his own thoughts and pre-established rules for long time. His wishes remained unfulfilled, he developed inferiority and sometimes started living with negative thoughts and adapted to the compromising view towards life. He becomes an opportunist, selfish and coward but in the later stages of life he gets all the desired comforts but he will never be satisfied.

Other Vipreet Rajyogas –

Saturn owns second and eleventh house so it is very beneficial in the condition of Vipreet Rajyoga especially if other evil or cruel planets also sits with him.

- Saturn in the second house and Mars in the eleventh house make the person earning very early in his age and by the time he reaches his youth he will become rich in life.

- Mars in the second and Saturn is either in eleventh or in the eighth house the person will be a millionaire for sure.

- Any two of the Saturn, Mars, Venus or Jupiter are exalted in the birth kundali the person will be rich even the exchange of houses in between any of these planets will make the person rich.

- If Mars in the eighth house and Sun in the seventh person will earn great wealth suddenly.

- Second house Venus and third house Mars makes a person very rich irrespective of his present financial position either he will take birth in a rich family or after his birth the family will become rich or he will be a self-made man anyhow he will earn great wealth.

- Saturn in the third house and Venus in the eleventh house makes the person rich with the help of family members.

- Sun and Saturn in the second or eleventh house makes the person rich through court or other legal measures.

- Mars and Ketu in the second house or Saturn and Ketu in the eleventh house makes the person suddenly very rich and he will have unexpected sudden gains many times in life.

- Mars in the seventh house and Mercury in the second house or Saturn in the seventh house and Mercury in the eleventh house makes the person rich after his marriage.

- Moon and Jupiter in 6th,8th or 12th house makes the person use others money.

- If both Mars and Venus are in the eighth house the person will be very rich all of a sudden and will receive unearned income.

- Mars and Saturn are in any of the houses together and connected with Jupiter then person will be rich.

- The person will start getting rich from the age of 28-32 years usually.

Points To Ponder –

- Vipreet Rajyoga in the Moon Chart or Chandra Lagna –

  If the Vipreet Rajyogas are not in the Moon Chart then the outcomes of Vipreet Rajyoga will be dropped down by 30%.

- Degree wise capability – If the evil planets in evil houses sits at the degrees under 6 or over 24 then the results will be best, always remember it is Vipreet Rajyoga not Rajyoga but there are me exceptions like if the degree of your ascendant's sign is 20 degrees and say if Sun sits in the eighth house with 17 degree or 23 degree it will still give good results as three degree either side of your ascendants degree the planets always fetch good results.

- Nature – It is Vipreet Rajyoga or opposite of Rajyoga so the person will behave opposite to his culture and family background like being a saint even after taking birth in a very rich family.

- Some bad yogas like KaalSarpa yoga can also end up in Vipreet Rajyogas so analyses these possibilities with sharp focus.

- Ketu is most important planet when we consider the long live fame in Vipreet Rajyogas.

- Rahu and Ketu if Co rules any evil house will act as Vipreet Rajyoga planets then the position of Saturn, Mars and Jupiter will become important.

- Saturn in the sixth house will give Vipreet Rajyoga irrespective of the sign it will be sitting in but yes the power of such Vipreet Rajyoga will depend upon the sign and position of Saturn in that birth chart. As it completes the evil circle it aspects sixth house, eighth house twelfth house and third house.

- Mars in the eighth house give Vipreet Rajyoga by covering the partial evil houses by its aspects, it see eighth house, eleventh house, second house and third house.

When you give everyone a voice and give people power, the system usually ends up in a really good place. So, what we view our role as, is giving people that power.

Mark Zuckerberg

His name needs not to introduce as everyone using Facebook the biggest social networking media site.

Mark Zuckerberg is co-founder and CEO of the social-networking website Facebook, as well as one of the world's youngest billionaires.

Born on May 14, 1984, in White Plains, New York, Mark Zuckerberg co-founded the social-networking website Facebook out of his college dorm room. He left Harvard after his sophomore year to concentrate on the site, the user base of which has grown to more than 250 million people, making Zuckerberg a billionaire. The birth of Facebook was recently portrayed in the film *The*

Social Network.

Zuckerberg developed an interest in computers at an early age; when he was about 12, he used Atari BASIC to create a messaging program he named "Zucknet." His father used the program in his dental office, so that the receptionist could inform him of a new patient without yelling across the room. The family also used Zuckberg to communicate within the house. Together with his friends, he also created computer games just for fun. "I had a bunch of friends who were artists," he said. "They'd come over, draw stuff, and I'd build a game out of it."

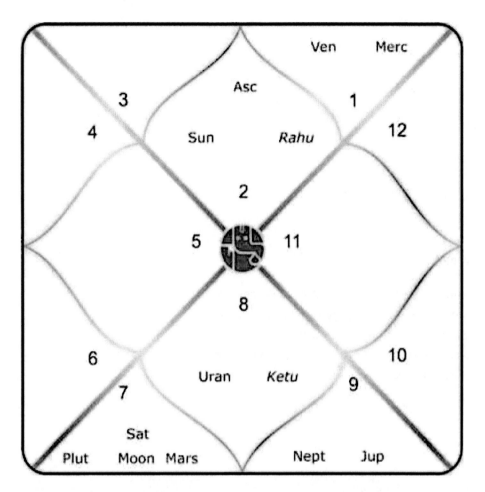

Who don't know Mark Zuckerberg the owner of the biggest social networking site Facebook today?

The strongest effect of Vipreet Rajyoga can be seen from his kundali and mind you this is his natal CHART has a good story to say but in bad words.

Nine Planets For Taurus Lagna/ Ascendants –

1. Sun –Rules fourth house
2. Moon – Third

3. Mars – Seventh and Twelfth

4. Mercury – Second and Fifth

5. Jupiter – Eighth and Eleventh

6. Venus – First and Sixth

7. Saturn – Ninth and Tenth

8. Rahu – Depends on Saturn and Jupiter Position

9. Ketu – Co rules house seven in this lagna for person.

Planets creating Vipreet Rajyoga for Taurus Ascendants

I had been on many articles and websites justifying the great success of this man as an outcome of intentionally created Rajyogas but the reality has a different tune to play. Simply look at his 6th,8th and 12th houses. All the lords of the evil houses are in the evil houses with evil planet like Saturn and conductive planet like mercury.

Lagna or Ascendant - Taurus

3rd house owner- Moon

6th house- Venus

8th house owner- Jupiter

12th house owner- Mars

Apart from them Saturn a naturally evil planet and Mercury lord of the partial evil house second and also an inductive planet which acts good with good and bad with bad.

Out of these four three are natural benefic planets now move to his conjunctions leaving the aspects or dristies.

3rd house- empty

6th house-

- If Mars comes into the sixth house- Person will gain hundreds and sometimes thousand times more than his efforts. He will have no enemies and gained money from foreign lands the only loophole is they are unlucky in the matter of spouse, either they will have to marry twice or their spouse will be sick or somewhat away from them

- Mars aspects twelfth house making his fame immortal and third house while sitting with the lord of the third house Moon and also the natural karka of third house the house of mass media and courage to take new ventures and these abilities are in abundance in Mark Zuckberg

- Moon lord of the third house, the house of courage, mass media and communication of controversial subjects is in the sixth house with twelfth house lord Mars and Saturn creating supreme Vipreet Rajyoga, the unique fact about the Vipreet Rajyoga created by Moon is it fulfills very quickly but if there are no other supporting Vipreet Rajyogas or even Rajyogas then its effect will be subsided quickly. Here Moon is getting the complete support from Mars and Saturn. Both are naturally evil and cruel planets. Moon also aspects the house of afterlife fame the twelfth house and hence increased the longevity of his name.

- Saturn – A Yogkaraka (the most beneficial planet) getting exalted in an evil house, this is very rare Vipreet Rajyoga hardly found in any chart. As a thumb rule of Vipreet Rajyoga says Saturn in the sixth house and Mars in the eighth house irrespective of the zodiac sign will give certain benefits as they completes the circle of evil through their aspects and Saturn is better in this.

Saturn, moon and mars so first come to Vipreet Rajyoga as Moon and

Mars or 3rd and 12th lords are together into the 6th house the results are very aggressive thinker he will sure engaged with personified females and earn maximum with minimum input because Moon optimizes the ego of Mars here remember Moon is the fastest moving planet and Mars is karka of work with Saturn here with Moon and Mars as Saturn conjunction with both Moon and Mars is adverse under normal circumstances but this is an adverse house and if Mars and Moon are together in Capricorn or Libra they always produce magnetic effect and same result will be if they join under a Vipreet Rajyoga condition the only bad outcome of this combination is that person will never be able to hide his secret relationships. Remember Saturn is exalted here so even a trine or quadrant lord if gets its exaltation in an evil house the result will be Vipreet Rajyoga.

8th house-Jupiter

Here Jupiter being 8th house lord is in its Mooltrikona sign very beneficial when a planet own either lagna and 8th house or 11th and 8th house creates Vipreet Rajyoga it give immense wealth for very long period of time and immortal fame as 11th house is for your worldly desires

If Jupiter is in the eighth house – The person will be highly respected, holds high morals and worshipped by the masses for centuries. His fame will live even after him and if Rahu sits with Jupiter his name will be all across the globe and if Ketu sits with Jupiter then he will attain Moksha or Nirvana or freedom from the circle of rebirth and he will be back to source energy or God.

12th house-Venus and Mercury-The specialty about Mercury is that it is a neutral planet if with benefic it behaves like benefic if with malefic it behaves like malefic and Venus is 6th house lord so there is parivartana or exchange of houses in between Mars and Venus and Venus magnifies the creative and communication quality of mercury here the result is

Facebook an endless route of communication created by him

ThIs kundali is one of the perfect examples of Vipreet Rajyoga as all the dus019sthana or bad house lords are in evil houses.

Point To Ponder –

Which Planet has the maximum contribution in the success of the owner of this Kundali?

It is the Saturn as its third aspect is on the eighth house, seventh aspect is on the twelfth house and tenth aspect is on the third house. Therefore it is a natural Vipreet Rajyoga when Saturn sits in the sixth house irrespective of the sign , here Saturn is exalted and sits with moon so he left away its biggest weakness the slowness.

Twelfth House – Contains partially evil lords Venus who owns sixth house and Mercury the second house, Mercury holds the first sign which is a natural Markesh or partially bad sign so it will also consider as an evil planet and Venus the only beneficial planet here but due to the combinations and aspects prevails in this particular birth chart Venus will also contribute in Vipreet Rajyoga specially when it is aspect by an exalted Yogkaraka, Saturn.

If Venus is in the twelfth house then the person will be victorious, lover, rich and good looking. He will live a perfect life till the end but if Mars sits with it, person will be sexually driven although he will be able to keep this secret but will give away money. He can be an owner of an NGO or any welfare society and will gain name.

Note -If Mercury and Venus combine in second, sixth or twelfth house the person will gain wealth through state or court for Taurus ascendants.

There is also a Parivartana Yoga or exchange of houses in between Mars and Venus.

A.P.J.Abdul Kalam –

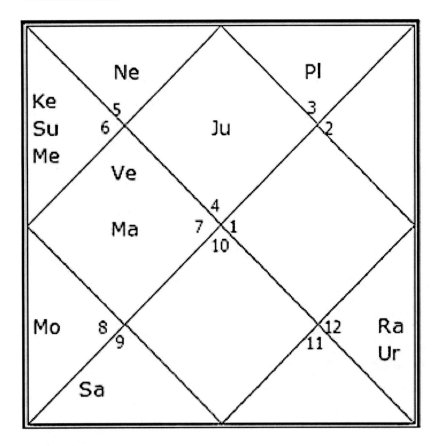

Lord of third house – Mercury which is also the lord of second house

Lord of sixth house – Jupiter which also holds ninth house

Lord of eighth house – Saturn

Other planets – Sun in the twelfth house

Here you can easily conclude in the third house there is Malefic Mercury and Sun owner of the second house and also magnifying the malfeasance of Mercury and Ketu increasing this effect several times more. Saturn in the sixth house aspects all evil houses the eighth, the twelfth and the third. Saturn in the sixth house is a natural Vipreet Rajyoga irrespective of the sign as it completes the full circle of all evil houses including his own sitting point in the kundali.

Dr. A.P.J. Abdul Kalam is most respected president of all times in the biggest democracy in the world India. He lived like a saint despite of no paucity of comforts and honor. A truly dedicated person towards his goals completely un moved by worldly pleasures.

Saturn in this particular birth chart makes the evil circle complete by its aspects on eighth, twelfth and third house.

Amitabh Bacchan –

I have never really been confident about my career at any stage.

Amitabh Bachchan

Yes these are the line by the most confident actor on the Indian silver screen Mr. Angry young man, Amitabh Bacchan, the superstar of the millennium and a person who's early life was full of rejections and failures and supreme level of struggle but once his career paced up it, still continuous defying his age and other time bounded attributes.

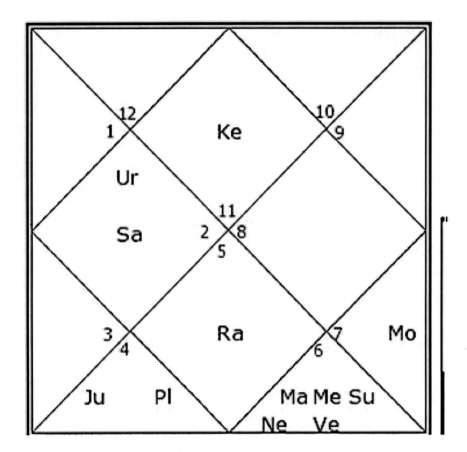

Mr. Amitabh Bacchan belongs to the Aquarius ascendant or Kummbha lagna the divine sign or punya rashi of Saturn and with well placed lord of the ascendant his birth chart or kundali is very remarkable as it contains the compound effect of Vipreet Rajyoga and Neech Bhanga Rajyoga (cancellation of weakness).

Nine Planets for Aquarius ascendants –

- Sun – 7th house
- Moon – 6TH house
- Mars – Owns 3rd and 10th house

- Mercury – Rules 5th and 8th House.

- Jupiter – 2nd and 11th houses.

- Venus – Lord of fourth and 9th house

- Saturn – Lord of 1st and 12th house.

- Rahu – Co rules house one

- Ketu – Temporary Lord of 8th and 10th house (only during his own time period.

Now let us analyze his chart to know the hidden force behind his everlasting success.

Sixth house –

Jupiter is in cancer in his exaltation sign and many will say it is a Rajyoga but what they forget is Jupiter is exalted in the sixth house and at the same time it is the lord of the 2nd house or pratham markesh or the first cause of threat to mortal life and he also rules the eleventh house, the house of gains but yet partially bad and it also qualifies under the circle of Vipreet Rajyogas.

From here Jupiter aspects 10th house giving numerous ups and downs to his career, twelfth house giving him fame beyond the mortal life and his own house the second house, the house of wealth, family, communication, liquid assets and hereby Jupiter increased these outcomes along with the life span of Amitabh Bacchan.

Eighth house –

Mars – Mars is an aggressive and naturally cruel planet and the first sign it owns is third house for this kundali and even in natural senses Mars is the karaka or most active planet in the third house. Here it is sitting into his enemy sign fanning the flames of Vipreet Rajyoga.

- Mars in eighth house makes a person, fastidious, brave, daring and he hardly consider anything important more than his own wishes and because of these qualities he becomes world famous. He very often puts himself in the spot of bother but he successfully tackles the hurdles in his way. Mercury also here adds the brain to his bravery and makes him little more diplomatic which helps him in increasing his popularity and wealth.

Mars from here aspects the eleventh house the house of wishes and a partially evil house, second house as discussed earlier the house of wealth and communication (no wonder why the aggressive dialogues from Mr.Amitabh Bacchan were so cool) and the third house , the house of courage and hard work and no one has the doubt on the level of struggle done by Mr.Amitabh Bacchan.

Mercury – Although the first sign owned by Mercury is divine but yet as per the thumb rule Mercury here exalted as the eighth lord or as an evil planet and reason is pretty simple it is sitting with Sun and Mars and both are naturally malefic planets and as per the adaptation qualities of Mercury it is bound to act as an exalted eighth house lord and due to which it is also creating very strong Neech Bhanga Rajyoga because Venus is getting weak in the same house in the sign of virgo where Mercury is getting exalted and hereby taking the best qualities of Venus which is entertainment, cinema, fame, luxuries and many more out but with considerable struggle.

Mercury in the eighth house makes an individual a world level speaker, artist, musician, actor, singer or musician. His fame goes beyond his mortal life. He places himself on the top of the ladder and gain the fame worldwide.

Mercury too aspects the second house from here and making Mr.Amitabh Bacchan much more diplomatic and artistc person and earning huge wealth because of his such abilities.

Sun – Sun as the lord of the seventh house and dritiya markesh or second threat for mortal life is forming Buddha Aditya Yoga taking Mercury as exalted and in its evil form enhancing the fame and money as it also directly aspects the second house.

So guys here is the real analysis of Mr.Amitabh Bacchan's birth chart and unleashing his secrets driven by the bad planets in his life.

Brett Lee-

He is a good guitarist and has a nice voice......

The above lines are for not any rock star or a melodious singer but for one of the fastest bowlers that world cricket has ever seen, yes these lines are for Brett Lee.

Brett Lee is recognized all through the Cricketing world as one of the fastest and most exhilarating speed bowlers to play the game. He has been recorded bowling at speeds of over 160km/h leaving batsmen with only a fraction of a second to counter once the ball leaves his hand.

Brett was born and brought up in Wollongong, New South Wales where he grew up with his relatives and their shared love of sports. Brett tried his hand at many sports but cricket prove to be the one that he excel in. He had his first authorized game of cricket at the age of nine.

Outside of Cricket Brett have many other interests. He has a love of music and has shaped the band White Shoe Theory and has in black and white a number of songs with his music partner, Mick Vawdon, for their album. Brett also launched in India with Asha Bhosle "You're the One" single, which he wrote the lyrics, and this went to the top of the Indian music charts.

Brett lives in Sydney and when at home he loves nothing more than spending time with his son 5 year old son Preston and family. Brett often also takes time out in his music studio or occasionally a spot of fishing on Sydney Harbour.

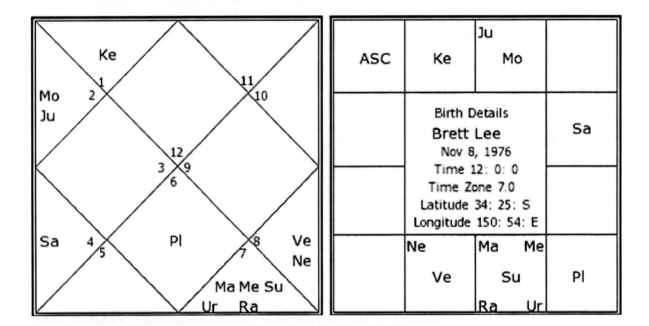

Look at his chart, may be the traditional astrologers claim that he has this Rajyoga and that Rajyoga but if you will have a bird's eye view at his Kundali you will again found good story but in bad words.

The most unique attribute of Brett Lee's chart is, he has close to NeechBhanga Rajyoga and Veepreet Rajyoga in his chart.

First of all he is a Pisces ascendant, the naturally soft and good looking individuals.

- Sun – Rules 6th house

- Moon – Owns 5th house

- Mercury – Rules 4th and 7th houses

- Mars – 2nd and 9th house

- Jupiter – 1st and 10th houses ruled by him.

- Venus- 3rd and 8th house

- Saturn – 11th and 12th houses

- Rahu – Co rules 12th house

Ketu – Subordinate ruler of 9th house

So now let us see what has made this music man a man of speed.

Third House –

Moon is exalted here and Moon is a lord of a trine and it is sitting here with Lagna lord or the lord of the ascendant Jupiter which also owns a quadrant 10th house but Jupiter is in its enemy sign. So exalted Moon with enemy Jupiter creates a special yoga or combination which lies somewhere in between Neech Bhanga and Vipreet Rajyoga.

Jupiter is in its enemy sign so bound to produce evil effect but how it comes to deliver good I will explain in proceeding lines.

Note – Both Moon and Jupiter are holding benefic signs and how they contribute to Vipreet Rajyoga will be explained in further lines.

Eighth House –

Mars – Although it holds a trine but it is a naturally cruel planet and the first sign it holds is second house the house of Pratham Markesh or first threat to life. And there is another thumb rule of Vipreet Rajyoga whenever Saturn sits in the sixth house it creates supreme Vipreet Rajyoga as it aspects 8th house, 12th house and third house, the complete circle of evil, likewise whenever Mars sits in the eighth house it aspects eleventh house, the house of gains and partially evil house, second house again a partially evil house and then third house again a partially evil house but somehow it completes the circle of evil in a partial manner so Mars has the capability to give second best Vipreet Rajyoga after Saturn, the intensity or strength depends upon the sign in which they sits in like if in enemy sign it will be the best, weak sign very good, neutral sign good. Here Mars aspect to third house or the house where Mars also holds the role of Natural Karka or the most effective planet from the house where he holds the position of the natural lord the eighth house forces Moon and Jupiter to produce the effect of Neech Bhanga Rajyoga because of the evilness of Mars.

Sun – Lord of the sixth house is in the eighth house and also it is in its **Debilitated sign which is creating a very strong Vipreet Rajyoga in itself. Aspecting the second house it creates the possibility of sudden fame and wealth.**

- Sun may not make person long lived but his life will be very healthy although proper remedies of Lagna lord if Lord of the ascendant is not strong must be done during the major and minor periods of other Markesh (Lord of the second and 7th house) to enhance life as Sun never be the cause of end for these persons. He will have great threat from fire and enemies and he may get great defeat from them. The fame will be great and person will gain money from his enemies and opponents.

Venus also makes the person long lived and the outcomes will get enhanced.

Here Sun denotes winner in the competition and for a competitive game like cricket such a combination is a divine blessing.

Mercury – As per the thumb rule Mercury is silent when it sits with Sun and as per its adaptation quality in the presence of cruel planets it also behaves like a cruel planet and it also holds the 7th house the house of the second Markesh or second threat to life and under very specific conditions the seventh house lords behaves in evil manner and one of those conditions is if seventh lord is in an evil house or in 6th,8th or 12th house with naturally cruel or evil planets like Saturn,Mars,Sun,Rahu and Ketu. Therefore Mercury here is creating supreme level of Vipreet Rajyoga.

Rahu – Naturally the most evil planet and co ruler of the 12th house in this birth chart speeds up the pace of Vipreet Rajyoga and because of this in the first half of the life of Brett Lee the effect of Mars was more than the effect of exalted Moon and he became a great cricketer.

As there is exchange Yoga in Between the third house and eighth house lord Venus and Ninth house lord Mars it also accelerates the pace of the outcomes in decent manners but as Mars is in neutral sign it can cause injuries to Brett Lee. The best house or the ninth house lord in the worst house or the eighth house and the worst house lord or the eighth house lord in the best house or the ninth house.

Albert Einstein –

Who doesn't know? Albert Einstein. The paramount of knowledge and father of theory of space and time.

Einstein was a Gemini ascendant

Nine Planets for Gemini ascendants –

- Sun – Rules the house of courage third house
- Moon – Owner or house second
- Mars – 6th and 11th house
- Mercury – 1st and 4th house
- Jupiter – 7th and 10th
- Venus - 5th and 12th
- Saturn - 8th and 9th
- Rahu - Co lords 9th house
- Ketu - Co ownership of 6th and 8th house

Let us examine why Albert Einstein enjoyed an everlasting fame which still continues today also the contribution of evil planets.

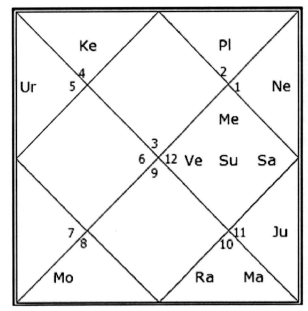

Sixth House –

It contains Moon the lord of the first Markesh or lord of the second house and that too in its debilitated form which is creating Vipreet Rajyoga related to Mind and if there had been no other combinations then Albert Einstein would have been a great doctor or inventor of some medicine. From sixth it aspects the twelfth house and making his fame last beyond his mortal life.

Eighth House –

Here is another classical example of compulsory Vipreet Rajyoga when Mars sits in the eighth house. Mars rules 6th and 11th houses and hereby proving to be a very strong subject for Vipreet Rajyoga on the following basis –

- As it is owner of one evil and one bad house that is 6th and 11th.
- It is getting exalted in the worst house of the Kundali in 8th house
- As per the thumb rule of aspect as it is sitting in the eighth house and from here it aspects eleventh house, second house and third house.

Mars owns sixth house in which Moon is debilitated and hence creating Neech Bhanga Rajyoga as owner of the sixth house Mars is exalted in another evil house, it is also a special kind of Vipreet Rajyoga.

Mars after being exalted aspects second house which rules by Moon which is debilitated in the house of Mars and hence it is creating another Neech Bhanga Rajyoga.

Mars also aspects the eleventh house which is also his own house and a partially evil house and the third house another bad house.

Rahu- Rahu here acts as a magnifier , although the co ruler of a trine but a malefic planet by nature and here sitting with Mars the most malefic planet of this birth chart and sitting in its Vipreet Rajyoga strength house and whenever Mars and Rahu comes together they create Angaraka Yoga which is most of the time an evil combination and a malefic combination by nature but here in this particular chart this Yoga is very beneficial taking the intellect of an individual to superior heights as eighth house also belongs to secrets, darkness , hidden sciences and Rahu here is acting as a substitute to Saturn and somewhat a super substitute which ultimately made Einstein greatest intellects of all times in the human history as Rahu also aspects twelfth house the house of beyond life that is why the theories of Einstein are still the subject of discussion and interest.

Another Neech Bhanga Rajyoga in this chart is debilitated mercury is joined by exalted venus, although not a Vipreet Rajyoga but Neech Bhanga Rajyoga also falls into the category of Non-Rajyogas.

Ketu which co rules sixth and eighth houses in this particular chart also sitting in a partially evil house the second house and Moon is getting neech (weak) in the sixth house and hence the evilness of the Moon is enhanced.

Emma Watson –

Emma Charlotte Duerre Watson

Date of birth - 15 April 1990 is an English artist, model, and campaigner. Watson rose to fame as her role <u>Hermione Granger</u> in the *Harry Potter* <u>film series</u> becomes admired, making her occurrence in all eight *Harry Potter* movies from 2001 to 2011 she climbed on the top of the ladder, surprisingly previously having acted only in school plays.[4] The contract earned Watson worldwide fame, serious accolade, and more than £10 million.

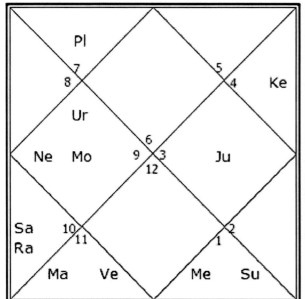

Born under the effect of Mercury and that too in its artistic form Emma has created wonders very early in her life and the basic cause of it is the placement of her Moon which owns the second house, the Pratham Markesh (First cause of death).

- Nine Planets for Virgo ascendant –
- Sun – Rules twelfth house
- Moon – Lord of eleventh house
- Mars – Lord or their and eighth house
- Mercury – Rules over first and tenth house
- Venus – Second and Ninth house
- Jupiter – Fourth and Seventh House
- Saturn –Fifth and Sixth house

- Rahu – Co rules sixth house

- Ketu – Co rules third and eighth house

Now let us analyze the placement of her evil planets in her Kundali or birth chart.

Her sixth house contains –

- Mars – Rules third and the eighth house and the most evil planet for this lagna or ascendant , sitting in the evil house and in neutral sign Mars as a natural cruel planet multiplies the effects of Vipreet Rajyoga to several times. With its seventh aspect it enhances the evilness of twelfth house in her birth horoscope.
- Venus – Although a naturally benefic planet but Venus is the cause of the soft death or first Markesh in this particular birth chart or kundali and contradictory to the rule of traditional astrology that the lord of the trine looses the bad effects of the evil houses is wrong as the first sign owned by Venus is second house and sitting with the most malefic planet Venus becomes partially evil for this house (evil or neech Venus gives several sex relations, money, many houses, luxuries but lack satisfaction, true love and many other satisfactory needs). Venus aspects the twelfth house and makes the fame everlasting beyond the life of an individual.

And the fourth and eighth aspects of Mars on the ninth house and on ascendant itself gives the pace to luck and personality development. Venus owns the house of wealth and communication and coupled up with fiery Mars it speeds up the gains and spreads up the fame.

Now we proceed towards the worst house of the Kundali or birth chart, the house of secrets, sudden ups and downs, sex relations, joint assets, fame and relations abroad, the eighth house.

It has the following planets sitting in here.

Sun - Owns the twelfth house, the house of final summary of life and the afterlife longevity of an individual's deeds. Sun is a naturally cruel planet and sitting in the worst house of the kundali. Sun aspects the second house the house of wealth and communication. There is a drishthi parivartan yoga or exchange of aspect in between Venus and Sun as Sun the lord of the twelfth house aspects second house and Venus the lord of the second house is aspects twelfth house and moreover Sun is in exalted sign and hereby magnifying the effect of Vipreet Rajyoga hundreds of times and providing grand success to Emma at such an early age.

Mercury – Although the lord of the ascendant yet Mercury is a neutral planet and will be benefic only if it sits alone and if with any naturally malefic or cruel planet the Mercury will also act like his partner planet and specially with Sun Mercury hardly has any say, therefore this birth chart is the classic example of Buddh Aditya Yoga in evil houses.

Ketu the co lord of the eighth house is also sitting in eleventh house magnifying gains with better speed. If you analyze the chart of Emma Watson she has just one placement good that is Moon in the fourth house apart from that its all the good game by the bad players even Saturn in his own sign is with Rahu and Saturn holds sixth house ownership and Rahu is the co lord of the same house the sixth house and hereby making Saturn denies its ownership of a trine the fifth house. This Kundali is a classic example of Vipreet Rajyoga.

Steve Jobs –

Everyone says they go the extra mile. Almost no one actually does. Most people who do go there think, "Wait...no one else is here...why am I doing this?" And they leave, never to return.

That's why the extra mile is such a lonely place.

That's also why the extra mile is a place filled with opportunities.

Be early. Stay late. Make the extra phone call. Send the extra email. Do the extra research. Help a customer unload or unpack a shipment.

Don't wait to be asked--offer. Don't just tell employees what to do-- *show* them what to do, and work beside them.
Every time you do something, think of one *extra* thing you can do...especially if other people aren't doing that extra thing.
Sure, it's hard. But that's what will make you different.

And over time, that's what will make you incredibly successful.

The above lines were spoken by one of the greatest elf made billionaire Steve Jobs.

Steve Jobs was the co-founder Apple Computers with Steve Wozniak. Under Jobs' guidance and management, the company pioneered a series of radical technologies, including the iPhone and iPad.

Steve Jobs was born in San Francisco, California, on February 24, 1955,

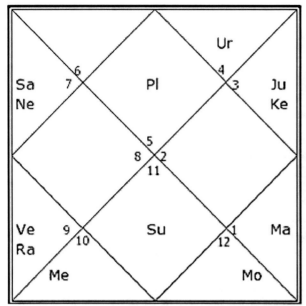

Here is the birth chart of the great man with innovative ideas and substantial achievements in his life.

Nine Planets for Leo ascendants –

- Sun – Lord of the first house or ascendant
- Moon – Rules 12th house
- Mars – Lord of fourth and ninth house
- Mercury – Rules Second and Eleventh house.
- Jupiter – Fifth and Eighth lord
- Venus – Third and Tenth lord
- Saturn – Rules sixth and seventh house
- Rahu – As per position of Saturn and Jupiter
- Ketu – Co rules fourth and Eighth houses

Let us see what his chart unfolds about his unleashed luck and abilities.

Third house —

Saturn in the third house creates supreme Vipreet Rajyoga as Saturn is a naturally malefic planet and it gets exalted in the house of courage, hard work, communication and other qualities related to working abilities of an individual and Steve Jobs had been an embodiment of hard work during his life. It aspects fifth house the house of children, education carrier in general, speculative gains, then it aspects ninth house, the house of luck and finally the twelfth house the house of the ultimate outcome of our mortal lives.

As Saturn rules both sixth and seventh house it acted as an effective shield for him in his life.

Saturn here will give good results related to third and twelfth house whereas bad results for trine houses it aspects. Exalted Saturn makes the person gain the good gains from third house like person will be very hard working will gain from brothers and friends and will have good communication abilities and as twelfth house positive results person will gain an everlasting fame.

Sixth house —

Mercury —

Rules two partially bad houses that is Second house and Eleventh house and here by giving mixed results. As second house is the house of wealth and eleventh house is the house of gains and desires, nobody has no doubt over the gains of Steve Jobs but as the Pratham Markesh or first planet to endanger mortal life Mercury sitting in the place of enemies, diseases, debts and all such bad entities the possibility of natural death was very little for him. Mercury from here aspects the twelfth house the house of expenses and health issues also but since exalted Saturn also aspects twelfth house this malefic effects nullifies to great extent and it enlarges the life span of Steve Jobs a little.

Mercury here making him money minded person who can earn from anything and everything.

Eighth house –

Moon – As the lord of the twelfth house moon in the eighth house or the house of sudden and uncontrollable events helps Steve Jobs to get support from authoritative persons both openly and secretly during his life.

Moon makes a middle age Yoga also but as the planet determines longevity is Saturn and it is exalted so this possibility declines for sure and life span increased. There is a cross dristhti parivartan yoga or cross aspect exchange yoga also in this chart where the lord of the second house Mercury aspects twelfth house and lord of the twelfth house Moon aspects second house.

Eleventh House –

Jupiter is in here creating Guru Chandal Yoga or Bramha Chandal Yoga as despite of the fact that the first sign hold by the Jupiter falls into a trine the fifth house, here Jupiter is sitting in a bad house the eleventh house and Jupiter also owns the worst house the eighth house in the kundali it is also in here with the co lord of the eighth house and a naturally malefic planet the tail of the serpent Ketu and hereby increasing the evilness of Jupiter.

And a very interesting fact if anyone observes that Jupiter aspects its arch rival Venus where Venus also holds third house and sitting with Rahu the head of the serpent and as per the position of Saturn Rahu also becomes the co ruler of the third house in this particular chart and hence increasing the flow of energy in between the two most creative planets and teachers Jupiter and Venus.

So Jupiter the ruler of the eighth house with co ruler or eighth house Ketu and Venus the ruler of the third house with the co ruler of third house Rahu,

J.K.Rowling was born to Peter James Rowling, a Rolls-Royce aircraft engineer, and Anne Rowling (née Volant), a science technician, on 31 July 1965 in Yate, Gloucestershire, England, 10 miles (16 km) northeast of Bristol.

Rowling has said that her adolescent years were miserable. Her home life was difficult by her mother's poor health and a stressed affiliation with her father, with whom she is not on speaking terms.] Rowling later said that she based the character of Hermione Granger on herself when she was eleven.

She had done many works but the lion's share of her success comes from her legendary work in fiction writing Harry Potter.

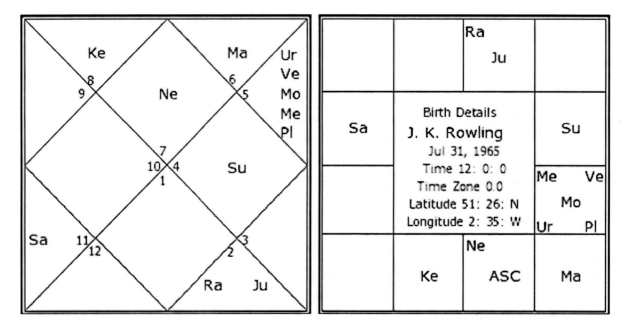

Libra the guys born to balance their lives and others lives too but some time they can be the balance changers also.

Nine Planets for Libra ascendants –

- Sun – Rules eleventh house

- Moon – Rules Tenth house

- Mars – Owns Second and Seventh house

- Mercury – Rules Ninth and twelfth houses.

- Jupiter – Third and sixth house Lord

- Venus – Rules First and Eighth houses

- Saturn – Rules Fourth and Fifth houses

- Rahu – Co rules Fifth house

- Ketu – Co rules Second house.

So let us move to analyze her evil houses and as the first house with the evil lord sitting in there is the eighth house ,the house of sudden events, transformation , secrets, magic, mysteries we first analyze that.

Planets in the eighth house are –

- Jupiter – Despite of being the most beneficial planet in Vedic Astrology it is the worst planet for this particular ascendant or lagna having the lordship of third and eighth house. So Jupiter the natural planet of luck and wealth and the natural Markesh or evil planet for Libra ascendant is sitting in the worst house the eighth house, in its enemy sign that is Taurus and sitting with naturally the most evil planet and the magnifier Rahu. Those who don't know much when Rahu or Head of the serpent and Jupiter comes together they tend to form Guru Chandal Yoga or Bramha Chandal Yoga, a very inauspicious Yoga or combination under the normal circumstances. But here this Yoga had been the depositor of the turn of fates for her. The most unique attribute of Guruchandal Yoga or when Jupiter and Rahu sits together or even Jupiter and Ketu comes together that they have common aspects, 5th,7th and 9th that magnifies the outcome either bad or good to exceptional extent specially whenever this yoga or combination happens to form while fulfilling the parameters of Vipreet Rajyoga.

Here the condition is same Jupiter from eighth house aspects the twelfth house the house for the fame of afterlife, after that it aspects second house the house of wealth , communication, family and the house of first cause of death and finally it aspects the fourth house. Therefore J.K.Rowling gains the benefits from the evil houses like twelfth and somewhat second also but the fourth house or the house of mother, satisfaction, stomach and many more. Those who knows about the childhood of J.K.Rowling they know she had disturbed childhood and the basic cause was the bad health of her mother and her bad relationships with her father and her early life struggles. Jupiter is planet of knowledge and sitting in the house of secret arts and knowledge which derived her to be such a good fiction writer moreover there is energy transformation combination in her Kundali or birth chart as there is a direct connection in between Jupiter ,Rahu and Ketu this combination has spelled the magic for her as Jupiter's aspects magnified by Rahu and Ketu transforms that energy to the sixth,eighth and tenth house because of which the full potential of sixth and eighth house was unleashed in her life but Sun in the tenth house becomes afflicted.

A partial and weak but still Vipreet Rajyoga is in her eleventh house where Moon,Mercury and Venus are sitting and due to the dual ownership of Venus and Mercury the gains will come to her but after a considerable struggle and delay.

J.K.Rowling-

Comparisons are really no good in sport, especially if it is a comparison between different eras and generations, for there are so many variables that come into play, starting from the quality of the opposition to playing conditions.

Sunil Gavaskar🔊

Sunil Manohar "Sunny" Gavaska born 10th July 1949 is an Indian past <u>cricketer</u> who played all through the 1970s and 1980s for the <u>Mumbai cricket team</u> and <u>Indian national team</u>. Widely regarded as one of the supreme <u>opening batsmen</u> in cricket history, Gavaskar set up the world records during his career for the most Test runs and most Test centuries scored by any batsman. He held the record of 34 Test centuries for almost two decades before it was broken by <u>Sachin Tendulkar</u> in December 2005.

Gavaskar was a Capricorn ascendant the ascendant of Sinners and contradicting the thumb rule of both Vedic Astrology which says the rise time of Capricorns comes after 32 years and Veepreet Rajyoga also because of his great early success he is one of the vital subjects of study for astrology scholars.

So our next Birth chart is of the first Indian Batsman who proved to be a myth breaker that Indian Batsman can't perform well on quick pitches.

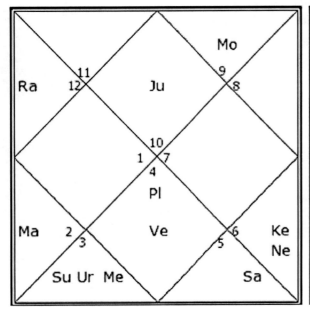

Nine Planets for Capricorn Ascendants –

- Sun Rules 8th house, the worst house
- Moon owns a partial bad house seventh house
- Mars holds fourth house and eleventh house
- Mercury holds 6th and 9th house
- Jupiter rules 3rd and 12th house and hence the worst planet for this lagna or ascendant.

So let our real analysis began –

Sixth house –

- Mercury in the sixth house makes the person successful with the dominant role of his enemies and his maternal relatives willingly or unwillingly. The enemies will be more a competitors rather than direct enemies and as the zodiac sign here is Gemini Mercury will fetch great benefits here. These persons generally have great and powerful enemies and they gain money and fame by defeating them and while competing with such giants they also sharpen up their intellectual skills with their hard work. Sun here creates strong Buddha Aditya Yoga and the outcomes of the mercury increased hundreds of times and person will become world famous player, athlete, brave and writer. Fame will be of worldwide level.

The planets sits in the sixth house aspects twelfth house and here by makes the fame of the person immortal.

- Mercury in the sixth house makes the person successful with the dominant role of his enemies and his maternal relatives willingly or unwillingly. The enemies will be more a competitors rather than direct enemies and as the zodiac sign here is Gemini Mercury will fetch great benefits here. These persons generally have great and powerful enemies and they gain money and fame by defeating them and while competing with such giants they also sharpen up their intellectual skills with their hard work. Sun here creates strong Buddha Aditya Yoga and the outcomes of the mercury increased hundreds of times and person will become world famous player, athlete, brave and writer. Fame will be of worldwide level.

Moon in the twelfth house makes the same magnifies his fame and make it everlasting.

So here we come to the one of the superhuman of the century Bruce Lee, a fighter, wonderer, actor and a person who had created a new paradigm of masculine marshal arts show THE BRUCE LEE.

From nowhere to everywhere was the reach of his fame and from dust his destiny raised him to the sky of fame and wealth.

Let us see his chart –

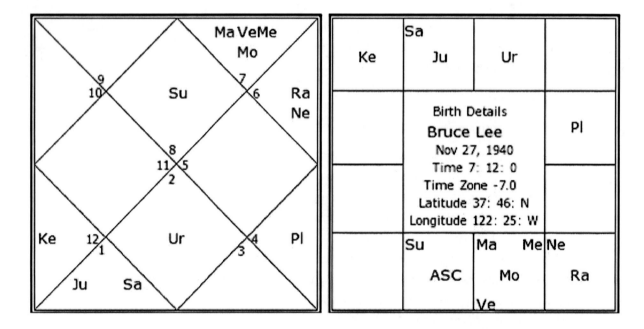

He was a Scorpio ascendant, an ascendant of supremacy, power and action and for Bruce Lee even these words are not enough for sure.

Nine Planets for Scorpio Ascendants –

- Sun – Lord of the 10th house

- Moon – Rules Bhagya sthan the house of luck 9th house

- Mercury – Lords 8th and 11th house

- Mars – Owns 1st and 6th house

- Venus – 7th and 12th house

- Jupiter – Rules 2nd and 5th house

- Saturn –3rd and 4th house

- Rahu – Co rules 4th house

- Ketu – Depnds upon the position of Mars and Jupiter.

Planets creating Vipreet Rajyoga –

- Mars- Being the lord of the ascendant makes Mars less effective in Vipreet Rajyoga but being naturally a cruel planet if he gets support of Saturn,Rahu,Ketu or Mercury then Mars can give complete outcome of Vipreet Rajyoga. It rules eighth house.

- Saturn – Rules 3rd and 4th house but being a naturally evil planet and arch enemy of Mars in Vipreet Rajyoga gives outstanding results.

- Mercury – Owns two signs 8th and 11th houses and with evil and cruel planets Mercury gives good benefits.

- Venus – Holds 12th house but own 7th house also and a naturally good planet so give mediocre results.

Third House – No Planets

Sixth house – Both the theories of Vipreet Rajyoga applies here as Saturn in the sixth house gives natural Vipreet Rajyoga by covering the circle of evil through its different aspects,

Sixth house Saturn is sitting, it aspects eighth house with its 3rd aspect, twelfth house with its seventh aspect and third house with its tenth aspect.

Moreover Saturn is in Aries in the sign of its Debilitation and hence increasing the outcome of Vipreet Rajyoga to its peak level.

Jupiter here also rules second house the Pratham Markesh (the cause of death) and sitting with Saturn it magnifies the effects of the sixth house.

Eighth House – No planets

Twelfth house – This is where the fame of Bruce Lee becomes immortal

Mercury which owns 8th and eleventh house becomes the most malefic planet for this particular birth chart. It aspects sixth house and Saturn and Jupiter aspects Mercury.

Mars lord of the sixth house and receiving full support from Saturn for creating Vipreet Rajyoga by both the placement and aspect of Saturn.

Mars itself aspects 3rd ,6th and 7th houses.

Venus the twelfth lord sitting in his own house and hence making the fame in cinema, movie, entertainment field immortal for Bruce lee.

Some people are born to play the different tune and create something innovative out of the pre invented streams and Jackie Chan is one of them.

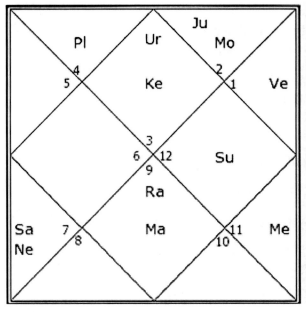

- Sun – Rules the house of courage third house

- Moon – Owner of house second

- Mars – 6th and 11th house

- Mercury –1st and 4th house

- Jupiter –7th and 10th

- Venus-5th and 12th

- Saturn-8th and 9th

- Rahu- Co lords 9th house

- Ketu- Co ownership of 6th and 8th house

Till now we have discussed the evil or bad lords in evil or bad houses but now we are going to do a Kundali with a little different type of Vipreet Rajyoga. In this particular natal chart Mars the lord of the sixth and eleventh house is in a quadrant the seventh house, Saturn owner of the eighth and the ninth house is getting exalted in a trine fifth house.

Moon the owner of the second house getting exalted in twelfth house.

Saturn aspects 7th ,11th and 2nd house all are partially evil houses but money making and public relation and partnership houses. And getting support from Ketu through its aspect and Mars is getting support from Rahu because of conjunction.

Henry Ford –

Born on July 30, 1863, near Dearborn, Michigan, Henry Ford shaped the Ford Model T car in 1908 and went on to progress the assembly line mode of invention, which revolutionized the industry. As a result, Ford sold millions of cars and became a world-famous company head. The company lost its market supremacy but had a lasting impact on other technological development and U.S. infrastructure

<table>
<tr><td>Ne</td><td>Pl</td><td>Ke</td><td>Ur</td></tr>
<tr><td></td><td colspan="2" rowspan="3">Birth Details
Henry Ford
Jul 30, 1863
Time 7: 0: 0
Time Zone -5.75
Latitude 43: 10: N
Longitude 85: 15: W</td><td>Me
Su</td></tr>
<tr><td>Mo</td><td>Ma
ASC</td></tr>
<tr><td></td><td>Ve   Sa
Ju</td></tr>
<tr><td></td><td>Ra</td><td></td><td></td></tr>
</table>

Nine Planets for Leo ascendants –

- Sun – Lord of the first house or ascendant

- Moon – Rules 12th house

- Mars – Lord of fourth and ninth house

- Mercury – Rules Second and Eleventh house.

- Jupiter – Fifth and Eighth lord

- Venus – Third and Tenth lord

- Saturn – Rules sixth and seventh house

- Rahu – As per position of Saturn and Jupiter

- Ketu – Co rules fourth and Eighth houses

Here the lord of Twelfth house is in the sixth Moon which gives fame beyond mortal life.

Lord of second and eleventh house is in twelfth house hence creating very beneficial Vipreet Rajyoga as both second and eleventh house denotes to material wealth and desires.

But what makes him super rich, literally rising up from the ashes of poverty to the paramount of wealth?

Look at the three planets sitting in his second house.

Venus, Saturn and Jupiter, one of the thumb rule in Vedic astrology is whenever these three planets sits together in whichever house or zodiac sign they always prove to be very beneficial in creating both Rajyogas and Vipreet Rajyogas.

Here they are sitting in Virgo a sign where Saturn is in friendly mode, Venus is Neech or weak and Jupiter in its enemy's sign.

House is second which denotes money , communication or vocal abilities, family.

Saturn is a natural Vipreet Rajyoga karka and in this birth chart it holds sixth house which is evil and seventh house which is

Markesh or evil under certain conditions. Saturn here aspects fourth house, eighth house and eleventh house.

Saturn although in its friendly sign but yet most natural Vipreet Rajyoga karna and it aspects 4th,8th and 11th house so two evil houses 8th and 11th.

Venus which is in its weak or necch sign Virgo and it aspects 8th house the worst house of Kundali and it increases wealth but also secret sex relationships for an individual as Venus here denotes sex and 8th house secrets. The first sign which Venus holds is 3rd house.

Jupiter is at its worst place as it is in its enemy sign and it aspects sixth house and it is also sitting with sixth house lord Saturn and although it also holds 5th house along with 8th but here it is in its enemy or worst sign so it will behave like 8th lord and it is aspects 6th house, 8th house which is also his own house, 10th house so here also it aspects sixth and 8th two worst houses.

Note –Second house got the conjunction in between the lords of sixth, third and eighth house and that too in dhana bhava or house of wealth and the houses covered by their aspect are 6th,8th and 11th house in which 8th house has maximum influence.

Moon in the sixth house and Buddha Aditya Yoga in 12th house with Mercury which owns second and eleventh house and aspected by 12th house lord Moon sitting in 6th house makes this birth chart as one of the most classic example of Vipreet Rajyoga.

All the planets own the evil houses or bad houses 2nd,3rd,6th,8th,11th,12th are somehow connected with each other and they are in the evil or bad houses it was not Raj Yogas which had made Henry Ford super wealthy.

Second house – Jupiter,Venus and Saturn

Sixth house – Moon lord of 12th house in sixth house

Twelfth house –Sun the lord of the ascendant and in its friendly sign but still in the sign of natural opposition of qualities as cancer is the sign of Moon which denotes water and Sun is a fiery planet so this placement is in auspicious for Sun and with Mercury which rules 2nd and 11th two bad houses it creates strong Vipreet Rajyoga along with Buddha Aditya yoga (sun and mercury together.)

Hope you have enjoyed this book and in the print version more birth charts will be included so kindly visit my page and give feedback to my work you can also mail me at mohitpandey0084@yahoo.com.

My Other Works

A Tale Of Ten Candles –

"Every time when you think that the light is removing the darkness, it is The Darkness which is capturing the light."

A group of teenagers enter an old cottage to seek refuge from the dangers outside hardly aware of the dangers that lurked within the walls.

Fueled by their curiosity, they decide to investigate the place. They discover an ancient chest that turned their lives around………………………

As the trunk is opened, what was inside it?, a treasure or a trap?

A long lost curse unleashes itself. Terrible curse that claimed the lives of many in the past, now thirsty for their blood…………

All they find are ten candles. Yes simply ten candles. Till these candles are burning there will be both Light and Life and if they extinguish there will be only Darkness and Death. Only true horror stories can save them because truth is life but this group of teenagers was playing this game for fun.

Will this fun become fatal for them?

Will they survive through an age old curse?

"A curse of tales"

"A tale of curses"

"A tale of ten candles"

Prologue –

"Hey look here what else I have found here," Avani quickly sauntered towards the dent in the opposite wall. And everyone followed her, Maahi was the last one to enter. It seemed to be a furtive place Meeta started checking out the pictures on the wall which were deemed to be very dull because of the substantial coat of dirt over it.

Maahi was looking down and slowly shifted his focus on the paintings and pictures on the wall. His eyes were glued on a picture of a lady with a long hat and full covered black dress when bbbbbhhhhhhhhaaaaaaaammmmmmmmm a hasty noise interrupted all of them. A big box had been dropped from the top of the roof.

All were stunned and silenced for few moments staring at that sudden surprise, whether from heaven or from hell? God alone knows.

"Hey it looks ancient and interesting too, let us open this," Harish marched towards that box.

"Curiosity killed the cat buddy don't touch that you can't expect to find a treasure here," Maahi's voice halted Harish.

"Ya he is right that box is very old and may contained dangerous bacteria or virus in it," Sujoy backed Maahi with seemingly logical words.

"Ohh you guys are too much this is just a simple box," Meeta moves closer to the box and started removing the dust covering it.

That was a big rectangular box carved with unidentified words and phrases all over it. It is so heavy Navomita tried to lift it.

Navomita,Karan,Amit and Meeta, all examined the box for over 15 minutes but to no avail.

How to open this piece of shit man, now Karan was also touching the box all around. The instructions here are in some cryptographic language." I think it is useless to waste time over it," Meeta stood up and moved away in frustration. "Let us move outside and check if the rain has been subsided by now," Roshni turned her back towards them.

As everybody started turning around Avani and Teena move close to that box and Maahi too was watching it closely for any clue to unlock it. They were turning it up and down and spreading their fingers all over it but nothing seems to be working when all of a sudden..........cclllliiinnnngggggggg the box cracked open by itself, may be while examining someone had pushed the unlock button..

"Oh Teena you did it," Avani shrieked, Teena remain stunned for a moment and then smiled.

"Mind you see....," Avani skewed towards Maahi while holding the hand of Teena.

"Guys its already just ten minutes to twelve now let us move back to our van as rain is also dwindled down now," Tony overlooked the opening of that box.

Yar Shambhu Kaka had clearly told us that he will be back around 3 O' clock what we will do while sitting and getting bore in that van let us have some adventure here may be we find really a treasure in this box," Sujoy lift open the box completely and others also joined him.

The box was very neat and clean inside. There were few papers and a black silk cloth wrapping something in it and a small box full of big matchsticks which were used long time ago around mid-60s.

"What is this bull shit making such a heavy wooden chest for reserving this silly garbage," Tony expressed in frustration.

"Hey what's under this?" Meeta quickly unfolded the black silver cloth.

Candles! they all exclaimed almost

together…..,1,2,3,4,5,6,7,8,9……..'Ten," Avani intervallic the counting of Meeta while standing at her back.

Facebook Link - https://www.facebook.com/A-Tale-Of-Ten-Candles-660646217335128/timeline/

Blog - http://attc084.blogspot.in/

Amazon - http://www.amazon.in/Tale-Of-Ten-Candles-Legends-ebook/dp/B00RZKRVV4

Favorite Sin

It is said that if you are mistaken once it's an error, twice its stupidity, thrice it's a habit and if even again then it's a Sin.

My destiny seems to direct me in the hunt of unknown and unexplored phenomenon, permanently it was supernatural energies and persistently it is love.

May memories were also like tears so they could have also dried up someday, but alas this is not possible, her memories making my life dry instead if drying up themselves.

Few things I have learnt in past few months about which I had different opinions earlier.

Mind is as much automatic as heart, no matter how much you try to divert it, it continues to insult your intelligence of practical understanding by giving empty emotions more priority.

Management and Love has one thing in common - No one can make you learn them. If something endures for long, it endures for a reason and it is this pain which is making me perfect.

Sometimes I feel like I have more break ups then affairs but all these break ups has built me up as a completely changed and charming individual.

In 9th standard I loved a girl Garima but she left me because she loved Rajeev our senior who played guitar well and she liked it. After her learned guitar and today it my guitar is not just an instrument but it is my extension, in higher secondary my girlfriend Sana left me for Ajit Singh he was a good boxer and after my break up I strain my every never and became better boxer than him and so on many girls left me because of some loophole in my personality and I work on to cover up those loopholes and today whatever I am, I am because of my break ups, I am rejoicing my life because of rejections.

My girlfriends have made me Kamina (Kami-deficiency, na-no) so Kamina for me is *jisme koi kami na ho* The perfect one.

Therefore Love May be a sin but it is my favorite one and this book Favorite Sin is a tale of twenty off beat love stories based on my personal experiences.

So enjoy the different shades of Love in Favorite Sin –

Facebook - https://www.facebook.com/Favourite-Sin-Love-838060722951227/timeline/

Blog - http://fs084.blogspot.in/

Negatives- Heroes not allowed

Hope, hate and love they all are both limitless and timeless. Negatives is a tale of timeless hope of hate to save limitless love no matter if to serve this purpose even the boundaries of births has to be broken countless times.

"They are back with different faces, different names and different identities but with same destiny, same desire and same detest, they are back, The Negatives are back", Yogi sprung up from his altar with a jolt.

"What happen Guruji (teacher)?, what happen?", all the young hermits came running to Yogi as it was unusual for them to see Yogi getting so excited and breaking his Samadhi (long meditation) so early.

"The oldest war of this universe will see its most unique turn of all times, they are back", Yogi's eyes had mixed expression of fear, fantasy and fatalness.

"What?" The faces of his disciples had a common mark of questions.

"This universe comes into the existence after the clash of matter and anti-matter and that fight is everlasting in the form of Devine and Devil, whenever any representative of the Darkness comes to rule the roost on earth, some Divine savior in the form of Messenger or Avatar comes to stop him, this is the rule but Satan has countless dices up his sleeve and every now and then he tries to surprise the nature, it's all preplanned for every Yuga (division of time in Hinduism)."

"In Sat Yuga (First phase of time) Lord Narsingha comes to kill Hiranyakashyapa, in Treta Yuga(Second phase of time) Lord Shree Rama incarnated to destroy great demon king Ravana, in Dwapar Yuga(third phase of time) Supreme Lord Shree Krishna had taken Avatar to destroy Kansa and other devil forces and in Kal Yuga (fourth and final phase of time) Lord Kalki will take Avatar to take on the ultimate war against kali(lord of the black holes) to destroy the darkness but if any dark force comes before the birth of Lord Kalki then?"

"But this will be the breach of the rule of nature Guru," one of his pupil uttered.

"Devil has already casted his dice hundreds of years ago son that rule has been broken", Yogi's voice shrilled.

"The God should also break the rules", his devotee replied in retaliating voice.

"No Satan can but God can't it will be against his own rules", Yogi reverted silently.

"Then what will be the solution?" all of them asked in group voice.

"Negatives, Negatives are the solutions and they are back, back after denying the death, destiny and dates, this time battle will be the most unique one, there will be no more Devil verses Divine but there will be *Devil verse Evil, Nocturnal verses Negatives,* but who will win The Heinous Devils or The Heartless Humans it's in the womb of time"., Yogi turn around and moved to his closet leaving everyone stunned.

Character overview –

Real Name -Bikram Dharmadhyaksha

Underworld Calls – Blind Death

"Death is blind it has no face, He kills so swiftly, that leaves no trace".
Bikram Dharmadhyaksha had tasted the worst poison within his mother's
womb when his father who was a professional samurai was killed by his
enemies and they forcefully made his mother drink poison when she was
pregnant.
To his stars his mother's father was an expert in ancient herbs in
Himalayan Mountains he saved his mother and him but Bikram was born
with a blessing and a curse. His body had

Natural resistances to any form of poison but his eyes were gone, he was
born blind but under the supervision of his father's mentor Pradyumna he
grown up as a death weapon and soon underworld started calling him
from Bikram Dharmadhyaksha to *Blind Death*.

Rumors say that his samurai can chop off even fire, water and air so
mortals are never on count but what about the immortals?

Real Name – Manohar Rakesh

Underworld Calls – Markesh (The cause of death)

Some calls him son of sea, others say he is a sea monster but the only
thing clear about Manohar was his father's name was Rakesh and he
was one of the greatest sea divers Mumbai had ever seen, Manohar
proved to be the chip of an old block and came to known as Manohar
Rakesh.
His hunt for money had drenched him into crimes along with water and
he started hunting sea creatures illegally, as the time passed he used to
smuggle prohibited goods through the most dangerous sea routes full of
sharks and other dangerous aquatic creatures.

The only good deed under his pocket was, nearby fishermen used to keep few drops of his blood with them so in any case of danger from sharks or other sea animals they unleash his blood inside the water, even sharks runs away after smelling it.

It was a proverb in Mumbai Docks that Markesh can breathe longer than fish, dive deeper than whale and hunt better than shark in water.

Real Name – Ishwar Chandra Upadhyaya

Underworld Calls – I.C.U., Faceless, Icchadhari (one who can take any form)

"His name was Ishwar, he had no face
He had one identity, he murder with grace"
In the mortal world the first identity on any individual is his face but he was faceless. It was a regular rumor inside the deserted and dark lanes of Mumbai Underworld that even mirror hasn't seen him.
Nobody knows from where he comes or where he goes; only the folktales of the high profile assassinations by him become his hallmark. He had warm desires and cold heart that's why the girls sleeps with him never wake up again. He left no traces behind him apart from a crushed rose near his prey.

As the underworld recognizes his skills, his name came to be recognized by several names like Faceless, I.C.U., Icchadhaari (One who can change his looks and form).

Real Name –Salman Qureshi

Underworld Calls – Salman Supari

"His nerves were of steel, his speed was fast,
He loved no sound apart from blast
His name was Salman but sir name was changed
Salman Supari was the name he gained"
The story of every human being is said to be written by God but some

humans are born to deny God's script. Babies sleep on listening Lori (song in India to let babies sleep) but he sleep after hearing the sound of crackers. When the sound of crackers turned into the sound of explosives no one had realized. Salman never asked anything from anyone even from the almighty but he snatched. He ditched his father, his people, his God, his country but honest to money.

Crime world often stated "it is not possible to give supari (contract) of God or Salman would have accepted that even". Nobody can save his opponents once he utter his favorite lines

"Jahapaana se haramipana" (mistake with the might)

Real Name – Dolly Deshmukh

Underworld calls –Dolly Dayaan

Her eyes were sharper than her Knives….

Her smile was nastier than her nails……….

Her lust knew one limit, the limitless sky….

Her heart had no emotions remains…

 She was known as Dolly Darling because of her charismatic charm and inevitable figure seductive enough to entice any opposite organ for her, but her beauty was the bait of the beast offered to hunt her prey and as the rate of the murders by her increased she gained a new name from her Mumbai Underworld fans –Dolly Dayaan (witch).

Her greatest ability under the rose of her beatific face was she was master of Black Magic and often uses her preys to enhance her dark powers.

What will happen when this merciless maid will face her worst fear THE BHAIRAVI?

Kindly visit my page to know about the other characters and sense the never ending battle of universe,

Negatives –

Facebook - https://www.facebook.com/Negatives-969362696429406/timeline/

Blog - http://negatives084.blogspot.in/

Vipreet Rajyoga (Amazing Astrology book one)

When we analyze the auspicious Yogas (Conjunctions, aspects and nakshatras in particular position) the first name comes to everyone's mind is Raj Yoga, Raj Yoga which led the person to live successful life with affluent resources at his disposal but when we go deeper into the Astrology secrets, men who merges his actions into the sea of fate and came out with unique pearls are very few. For example-Lord Buddha, Napoleon, Alexander the great, Mahatma Gandhi, Mark Zuckberg , Sachin Tendulkar and many more who just turned their fate around and reached hundreds and thousands times over and above their previous level are very few whereas Raj Yogas you can found in the Kundalis of lacs and lacs of people.

So, where lays the difference?

It indicates that there are certain Yogas in Vedic Astrology which are not only beyond Raj Yogas but also far more powerful and highly active than them, they have ability to take a normal human to outstanding level and a good for nothing individual to best for everything stage and major of such yogas are-

First - Neech Bhanga Raj Yoga (Cancellation of Weakness)

Second – Vipreet Raj Yoga (Turn of Fates or Reversal of fortune)

It was both a bit shocking and surprising for me that on internet there are countless articles available which explains Neech Bhanga Rajyoga and its attributes and effects but almost everywhere Vipreet Rajyoga has been considered as a mere stroke of luck and some half logics like Vipreet Rajyoga needs to have supporting Rajyogas to sustain the success and blah blah blah whereas the reality is this that Vipreet Rajyoga has all the qualities of Neech Bhanga Rajyoga with couple of additional advantages over it- It brings great success without much efforts or no efforts at all and it brings success timely unlike in Neech Bhanga Rajyoga where the person although gets great success but after a long and hard struggle.

This book contains the in depth analysis of Vipreet Rajyoga concept with its applications in different lagnas (ascendants) and with example of analyzed kundalis of great persons having this unique Yoga in their Kundalis.

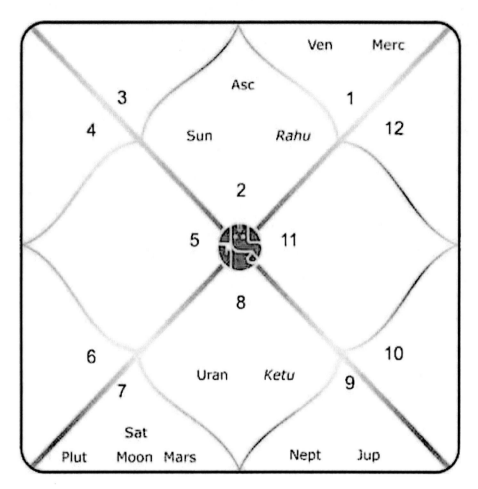

Who don't know Mark Zuckerberg the owner of the biggest social networking site Facebook today?

The strongest effect of Vipreet Rajyoga can be seen from his kundali and mind you this is his natal CHART has a good story to say but in bad words.

Nine Planets for Taurus Lagna/ Ascendants –

1. Sun –Rules fourth house

2. Moon – Third

3. Mars – Seventh and Twelfth

4. Mercury – Second and Fifth

5. Jupiter – Eighth and Eleventh

6. Venus – First and Sixth

7. Saturn – Ninth and Tenth

8. Rahu – Depends on Saturn and Jupiter Position

9. Ketu – Co rules house seven in this lagna for person.

Planets creating Vipreet Rajyoga for Taurus Ascendants

I had been on many articles and websites justifying the great success of this man as an outcome of intentionally created Rajyogas but the reality has a different tune to play. Simply look at his 6th, 8th and 12th houses. All the lords of the evil houses are in the evil houses with evil planet like Saturn and conductive planet like mercury.

Lagna or Ascendant - Taurus

3rd house owner- Moon

6th house- Venus

8th house owner- Jupiter

12th house owner- Mars

Apart from them Saturn a naturally evil planet and Mercury lord of the partial evil house second and also an inductive planet which acts good with good and bad with bad.

Out of these four three are natural benefic planets now move to his conjunctions leaving the aspects or dristies.

3rd house- empty

6th house-

• If Mars comes into the sixth house- Person will gain hundreds and sometimes thousand times more than his efforts. He will have no enemies and gained money from foreign lands the only loophole is they are unlucky in the matter of spouse, either they will have to marry twice or their spouse will be sick or somewhat away from them

• Mars aspects twelfth house making his fame immortal and third house while sitting with the lord of the third house Moon and also the natural karka of third house the house of mass media and courage to take new ventures and these abilities are in abundance in Mark Zuckberg

• Moon lord of the third house, the house of courage, mass media and communication of controversial subjects is in the sixth house with twelfth house lord Mars and Saturn creating supreme Vipreet Rajyoga, the unique fact about the Vipreet Rajyoga created by Moon is it fulfills very quickly but if there are no other supporting Vipreet Rajyogas or even Rajyogas then its effect will be subsided quickly. Here Moon is getting the complete support from Mars and Saturn. Both are naturally evil and cruel planets. Moon also aspects the house of afterlife fame the twelfth house and hence increased the longevity of his name.

• Saturn – A Yogkaraka (the most beneficial planet) getting exalted in an evil house, this is very rare Vipreet Rajyoga hardly found in any chart. As a thumb rule of Vipreet Rajyoga says Saturn in the sixth house and Mars in the eighth house irrespective of the zodiac sign will give certain benefits as they completes the circle of evil through their aspects and Saturn is better in this.

Saturn, moon and mars so first come to Vipreet Rajyoga as Moon and Mars or 3rd and 12th lords are together into the 6th house the results are very aggressive thinker he will sure engaged with personified females and earn maximum with minimum input because Moon optimizes the ego of Mars here remember Moon is the fastest moving planet and Mars is karka of work with Saturn here with Moon and Mars as Saturn conjunction with both Moon and Mars is adverse under normal circumstances but this is an adverse house and if Mars and Moon are together in Capricorn or Libra they always produce magnetic effect and same result will be if they join under a Vipreet Rajyoga condition the only bad outcome of this combination is that person will never be able to hide his secret relationships. Remember Saturn is exalted here so even a trine or quadrant lord if gets its exaltation in an evil house the result will be Vipreet Rajyoga.

8th house-Jupiter

Here Jupiter being 8th house lord is in its Mooltrikona sign very beneficial when a planet own either lagna and 8th house or 11th and 8th house creates Vipreet Rajyoga it give immense wealth for very long period of time and immortal fame as 11th house is for your worldly desires

If Jupiter is in the eighth house – The person will be highly respected, holds high morals and worshipped by the masses for centuries. His fame will live even after him and if Rahu sits with Jupiter his name will be all across the globe and if Ketu sits with Jupiter then he will attain Moksha or Nirvana or freedom from the circle of rebirth and he will be back to source energy or God.

12th house-Venus and Mercury-The specialty about Mercury is that it is a neutral planet if with benefic it behaves like benefic if with malefic it behaves like malefic and Venus is 6th house lord so there is parivartana or exchange of houses in between Mars and Venus and Venus magnifies the creative and communication quality of mercury here the result is Facebook an endless route of communication created by him

This kundali is one of the perfect examples of Vipreet Rajyoga as all the duststhana or bad house lords are in evil houses.

Point to Ponder –

Which Planet has the maximum contribution in the success of the owner of this Kundali?

It is the Saturn as its third aspect is on the eighth house, seventh aspect is on the twelfth house and tenth aspect is on the third house. Therefore it is a natural Vipreet Rajyoga when Saturn sits in the sixth house irrespective of the sign , here Saturn is exalted and sits with moon so he left away its biggest weakness the slowness.

Twelfth House – Contains partially evil lords Venus who owns sixth house and Mercury the second house, Mercury holds the first sign which is a natural Markesh or partially bad sign so it will also consider as an evil planet and Venus the only beneficial planet here but due to the combinations and aspects prevails in this particular birth chart Venus will also contribute in Vipreet Rajyoga specially when it is accepted by an exalted Yogkaraka, Saturn.

If Venus is in the twelfth house then the person will be victorious, lover, rich and good looking. He will live a perfect life till the end but if Mars sits with it, person will be sexually driven although he will be able to keep this secret but will give away money. He can be an owner of an NGO or any welfare society and will gain name.

Note -If Mercury and Venus combine in second, sixth or twelfth house the person will gain wealth through state or court for Taurus ascendants.

There is also a Parivartana Yoga or exchange of houses in between Mars and Venus.

Amazing Astrology –

Facebook Link - https://www.facebook.com/aa084?fref=ts

Amazon - http://www.amazon.in/Vipreet-Rajyoga-Unleashed-
Amazing-Astrology-ebook/dp/B015M1SNC8

Blog - http://aa084.blogspot.in/

Beyond Lights –The darkness knocks

Why a gentry so called contemporary people, overlook the supernatural
powers particularly Satan in the universe and they also consider the
believers in him as a biggest fool in the world." But these civilized
people needs to go back to their text books of science in the school to
get the right answer.

As per the quantum mechanics we recognize that each atom needs to
be steady by either giving or taking electrons or sub-atomic particles to
maintain the equivalence between negative charge and positive charge
is must for the stability and there are some neutral charges presents as
well.

Similarly in this universe also governs on the same law, we have:

1. GOD as a divine energy or positive energy or positive charge.

2. Satan or the dark energy or the negative charge.

3. Humans or the mediums of connection to complete the circuit or the
neutral charge.

The same texts we get in almost all our Vedas and Puranas that the
bases of all matter in this universe are three –

.Satva The Divine

.Tam The Devil

.Raj The Human

And this identical circulation of progressive and negative powers makes
our world constant. If there is a positive entity God then his negative

must also be here. It is a real surprising phenomena that a lot has been written on God and his representatives like prophet ,avatars and many more but the most strong and the contrary force in nature has been ignored he is Satan. In this book I have tried to define his nature, importance and role in this universe.

This book explains the scientific and religious explanations of Satan which were before used to explain God only, its relation with God and its ultimate aim and most important why Humans are so vital for both God and Satan

Facebook Link - https://www.facebook.com/beyondlightsthedarkness?fref=ts

Blog - http://bltdk.blogspot.in/

Amazon - http://www.amazon.in/Beyond-Lights-The-Darkness-Knocks-ebook/dp/B00IPJR2HW

Beyond Lights – Shadows of the Darkness

God and Satan. But who is more powerful this phenomenon is still under the rose.

They say Light but I favor Darkness. No matter how far light goes where light reaches its limit darkness starts. No matter how large the diameter of light is, it is always enclosed in the Darkness. All the sources of light are limited weather it is a small lamp which lasts for few hours or Sun which continues for several billion years but at the end it will be the darkness which will win the race. Darkness is source less and endless and ever prevailing in this universe. Before the genesis of light there was darkness and after the extinction of light there will be darkness. Darkness was never born and will never end it is Omni present and ever present for creation of light darkness is essential. You can create light in darkness but you can never create darkness in light.

Since very ancient times we are having representatives of darkness and light coming into this world in the proportion of their power and influence in this world and one can easily sense the ever increasing influence of the dark forces if go through the history. The sins are increasing; the darkness is expanding its sphere with every passing day. We have representatives of God right through the history. Shree Rama, Shree Krishna, Great Prophet, Holy Jesus from the darker front we have demons like Ravana, Kansa, Hitler and many more but these representatives are different more powerful that's why noticeable but in our day to day life and even after life we all are their representatives.

My last book was about God and Satan and this book is about their forces. Many and many books had been written in the past and will be written in the future on the representatives of Divine but has someone ever thought about the dark forces of nature. Think about these questions for few seconds –

- How Ghosts are different from Humans?
- What is the Bio-atomic structure of Ghosts?
- How Chudails and Daayans are different?
- Is Bhoot and prêt are same?
- Is Pisaccha is the east version of vampire from west?
- Why Betaal or Vetaal is more dangerous?

Do these questions tickle your mind? If yes then you are at the right junction.

This book is dedicated to the ever present power in the Universe and Its representatives, this book will reveal the darker side of the divine or the divine side of the dark, this book is about the darkness and its shadows or representatives in our world.

Charity begins at home so genesis of this series will be from my birth nation India. A country of various coulters, religions and races and this is not alone it is coupled with dark cults and forces still active at many places and the secret genre of evil is still continuing.

Inside this book you will find the differences and specific attributes of common race of evil, just like all humans are same all across the globe basically but there lays differences so as these visible forms of dark energy are same from roots but yet have significant differences.

Beyond Lights – Shadows of the Darkness

Facebook Link - https://www.facebook.com/Beyond-Lights-Shadows-Of-The-Darkness-631739473572697/timeline/

Blog - http://sotd084.blogspot.in/

Amazon - http://www.amazon.in/Shadows-Darkness-Beyond-Lights-Book-ebook/dp/B00J0FEIUE

Chalte Chalte –

Even the most beautiful days has their own sunsets and the darkest nights their sunrise, the only thing which is permanent is your temperament with which you enjoy the good days and see off the tough times in your life.

Very often guys asked me that how I manage to retain a good academic record along with my writing and business, I have got a very simple answer, I never think about the things which are beyond my control. For example I am writing this article without thinking that weather you guys will like it or not because it is something which is well beyond my control, what I can do is try to write the best possible article.

It is not only this article but in every arena of our lives as most of the times we deny to do things which we like just because of the fear of the factors beyond our reach like- weather I will be able to clear competitive exam, will she accept my proposal, weather my friends or relatives will accept this and many other things where we deny the very first step just because of the fear of the second step.

Guys also asked me weather I believe in hard work or destiny and you can call my answer a bit equivocal as I believe in both as hard work provide us capability and destiny serves us with a chance and only a capable person can utilize a chance.

With talent opportunity is a waste and without opportunity talent will be lying on the shelf so if your time is running hard now then even never deny your determination towards your efforts.

Always remember even a barren land deprived of rain for decades takes a single shower to bring its life back and a long period of failure and struggle will take a single stroke of success to change your life but when that stroke of luck hits you, you should also be capable to negotiate it well to serve your purpose.

The problem with those guys who curse their destiny is they started depending on luck rather than trusting it. Depend on your hard work and trust your luck that's they only way to go. There is nothing like Luck vs Hard work in fact it is Luck and Hard work, they both are counter parts of success luck generates chances and hard work cashes them it is as simple as that.

But yes I always give a little edge to efforts over luck. It is said is lucky the one who strike the iron when it is red hot and hardworking is the one who makes the iron red hot by continuously striking it so a man committed to his aim and consistent with his efforts will surely change his luck one day or another.

Sometimes I feel upset whenever I see stupid posts on social media where guys compare their religions and indulge themselves into the aimless arguments. If I will start hating God someday than it will be because of the religions. Apart from his countless creations it is the religion which gives me a solo reason to hate him this may be because it is not created by him.

God vs Religions this seems to be the scenario these days and to my wonder religions seems to be winning the battle but I have opted for the loser's corner, the corner of God and God too seems to be backing my choice as religion fanatic people only end up in a fruitless, enjoy less and stressed lives only producing destruction and gaining hate from the world.

I don't want to contradict any belief but the very true thing is this that on the behalf of those religious books these people define various varieties of Gods those books can't define a simple theory of gravity, they call him by several names Bhagwaan,Allah,God etc. but I have a single and most suitable name for him "Limitless".

No book,no religion, no messenger or avatar can define his power he is beyond the mortal limits. If you want to really feel God than feel his greatness as he never discriminate in between humans by giving sunshine, water and everything without asking our races.

It is not the end of days which will destroy the earth it will be the end of humanity. God only creates it is we who destroys weather forests or rivers or each other it is foolishness to blame God for everything.

It is humans who fail to consider other humans as humans not God or his creations.

Winner is the one who had failed more times than the looser had tried, this is the most logical definition of both winner and looser as per me.

Some are born perfect and some are born to be perfect with their own efforts and zeal.

Always remember one thing weakness is nothing but your own will so as your strength and there is no weakness in a human which he cannot convert into his strength at his will.

I had read somewhere a very interesting quote-

True friends are like stars they may not be close to you but always with you when you need;

But I think my sky is out of stars so I have decided that it is better to count on yourself than on stars and this is the key mantra of success, it is only you who can take out the best in you the only matter if fact is sometimes circumstances are the cause of it and other times your own choice.

For example few years back I didn't knew cooking but when I had to cross the domestic borders and face food problems as vegetarian food which was hard to find (As I am vegetarian) I had no choice but to cook by myself and now I can pace up with any five star hotel cook in more than few dishes, it was the condition which removed my weakness.

When in school I often wake up late for my boxing classes but slowly I developed this habit of waking up early (although it was a hard nut to crack) and today even I am early bird to answer the morning call, so here my choice was the cause behind the conversion of my weakness into my strength.

Sometimes you succeed and other times you know to develop a better strategy, failure is nothing but an illusion of weak minds and non-committed hearts.

When I was in B.B.D. Lucknow one of my X- Gf had told me 'try try till you succeed' and girlfriend vanished with time but not these words in fact this is the only thing I remember about her.

Always have big heart to gain big success in life, big heart is not the one which enjoys big success but big heart is the one which can sustain great failures.

Deceived by friends or ditched by lover just remember one thing when nobody backs you up, back up yourself.

I am ok with a broken heart but I will be done with a broken courage.

Dil toote to toote Himmat nahi tootni chahiye (Never allow your heart break to break your courage).

Thanks for your concern about my upcoming horror thriller 'Negatives' soon my book will knock the market.

Always yours love you all.

Facebook Profile –

https://www.facebook.com/mohit00087

Facebook official fan page –

https://www.facebook.com/mm084?ref=aymt_homepage_panel

Twitter Profile - https://twitter.com/mohitpandey1984

Official Blog - http://mm084.blogspot.in/

Instagram - https://instagram.com/mohit00084/

Wikipedia - https://en.wikipedia.org/wiki/User:Mohit8957

E-Mail – mohitpandey0084@gmail.com

CPSIA information can be obtained
at www.ICGtesting.com
Printed in the USA
LVOW09s1924121017
552179LV00020B/147/P